Dear Mark,

# Heart Touchers

Life-Changing Stories of Faith, Love, and Laughter

May these stories touch
your heart in a very
special way and may
they always remind you
of what is really
important in life...

Michael T. Powers

Galatians 2:20

# Heart Touchers

Life-Changing Stories of Faith, Love, and Laughter

**Michael T. Powers**

# Table of Contents

# About the Author

Michael T. Powers resides in Southern Wisconsin and is happily married to his high school sweetheart, Kristi. Their stories appear in 21 different inspirational books including many in the Chicken Soup for the Soul series. They have three precious boys: Caleb, Connor, and Chase who provide an endless source of heartwarming stories. Michael is the Youth Pastor at Faith Community Church in Janesville, Wisconsin, owns a video production business (Video Imagery), coaches high school girls' sports, and is the founder of HeartTouchers.com and Heart4Teens.com, which are free e-zines that feature inspirational and uplifting stories by published writers. To subscribe to HeartTouchers or Heart4Teens and join the thousands of world-wide members in their e-mail family, send a blank e-mail with the word "subscribe" in the subject line to: HeartTouchers@aol.com, or join through their website at: http://www.HeartTouchers.com

Michael and Kristi would love to hear from you! Feel free to let them know what you thought of this book or perhaps comment on how a particular story may have touched your heart! E-mail Michael at: HeartTouchers@aol.com and Kristi at: NoodlesP29@aol.com. You can write to them at:

Michael and Kristi Powers
Faith Community Church
2931 Lucerne Dr.
Janesville, WI 53545

Michael is also a motivational speaker and can be scheduled for your next adult or teen event by contacting him at: HeartTouchers@aol.com.

# Acknowledgements

This book is dedicated to the memories of Richard L. Conway, Edith Kelsey, and "Mr." And "Mrs." Eddie & Irene Sommers. But most of all to "Krissie." Kristi: You are the love of my life and song of my heart. Thank you for always believing in me, always expecting the best of me, and most of all, for waiting for me to grow up...

So many people to thank...To Caleb, Connor, and baby Chase, thank you for making every day feel like heaven with your hugs, kisses, and giggles. To Jeff and Christina Miller, Steve and Heidi Paulson, and Sarah Stone, thank you for your life-long friendship and for knowing everything about me yet loving me anyway. To Carole & Bart Merwin, Janet & Roy Hahn, Gary & Debbie Kelsey, Rick, Jana, Kayla & Jordan Conway, Jennifer Pozzani, Kim Conway, Kathy & Emily Pann, April, Jim, & Paul Greenwell, and the extended Conway and Kelsey families for your love and support through the years and for helping to hold my marriage together. All of you will never know how much you mean to my family. To Bill Greer and April Greenwell, thank you for making me believe that what I wrote was worth reading. To authors Joan Wester Anderson, Alice Gray, Allison Gappa Bottke, and Yitta Halberstam, thank you for your endless patience and for taking this writer under your wings. Your encouragement kept me believing in myself. To Lee Simonson of Heartwarmers.com and Azriela Jaffe, thank you also for your encouragement and for opening endless doors for my writing. To Karen Mullen, my high school teacher and now my editor, thank you for taking on this project and for what you have meant in my life. Special thanks also to Steve Markgraf for his invaluable help in copyediting.

To those people in my life who make facing each day a joy. To Brittnia Brandl, Kristin Monroe, and Jamie Rusch, thank you for the incredible love that you have shown us, for taking an interest in our children, and for always going above and beyond the call of duty. (Be wary of ice-cubes Brittnia!) To Aunt Rose Ellen, Darla and Lindsey Monroe, Trisha LaCoste, Tim, Linda, Samantha, and Abbey Holcomb, Lisa Kinkaid,

Jillian Lucas, Renee' Nodorft, Rebecca Ligman, Megan Stevens, Emilie Hanson, Raquel & Janeka Stilwell, Julie Opperman, Maren Miller, Gena Gilbertson, Tricia Statton, Carlynn Zahn, Becky Nilson, Bridget DeLong, Laura Madson, Sara Douglas, Brandi Williams, Kelsey Marx, Trisha Scott, Ami Peterson, Stacey Blue, Diedra Mueller, Kristin DeLong, Sarah Gracyalny, Kim Boudreau, Danielle Hahn, Aundrea Fleck, Jena DuCharme, Al & Lori Bower, Dennis & Prudence Miland, and Samantha Risseeuw, thank you for all the love and encouragement you have sent our way! Special thanks to the Beals, Blue, Boudreau, Brandl, DeLong, Hanson, Korth, Ligman, Lucas, Marsden, Marx, Miller, Mueller, Nilson, Pratt, Roach, Rusch, Schultz, Schwandt, Scott, Splan, Splinter, Statton, Stevens, Stone, Uppenkamp and Wellnitz families. Pastor Jeff Williams and Colleen Hansen, thank you for modeling true leadership.

To the Madison P&DC gang: Angie Nelson, Jeff McHugh, Michael Young, Jeff Schultz, Sandy Owen, Nick Kunkel, Lee Roth, Larry Held, Janice Miller, Kenn Chavez, Chris Buxton, Steve Markgraf, James Campbell, Andrea Lewison, Renata Archambault, Barbie Moorhouse, Kelle Dunn, Stacey Bonilla, Mike and Andy King, Mark Flynn, Goldie Bristol, Paul Byers, and Susan Wedeward, thank you for making my years with the USPS an enjoyable experience!

To Charlene Kephart, Terri McPherson, and Saga Stevin, thank you for reaching across the miles and touching us in a special way. To Rod & Nancy Sawyer, Dennis & Debbie Roach, Roger & Twyla Johnson, Larry & Sue Bresser, Gary & Sue Beeman, Randy & Kathy Loescher, and Dan & Becky Thompson: thank you for being our role models and mentors. To Rich and Tina Napper, we may not say it often, but there are few couples we respect and admire more than you two. To Pastor Jeff Williams and Brenda, Pastor Sean Christensen and Heather, Janet DeRosier, Jonanne Manogue, and Pastor John Billow and Carol, thank you for your friendship, but more importantly for "feeding" us spiritually. To Jonanne Manogue and Brenda Williams, thank you for teaching my children about Christ's love in such a meaningful and creative way. There is no one I would rather have teaching my children about God's Word! To Matt and Kristi Kauffman, Rachel and Kent Martin, and Tedi Knox for your deep friendship, unerring loyalty, and for unselfishly giving of your time to help make a difference in the lives of teenagers. To all our youth ministry students, thank you for placing God first in your life and allowing Him to take care of the rest...

To Mary "Jazz" Jaskolski, Jay Potter, Bruce & Karla Chrislaw, Dee Horn, Michelle Smith, Brian McGuigan, Erin Dezwarte, Kaaryn Hermsen, Randy, Rita, & Ron Stelpflug, Pete & Michelle Keffer, Carrie Ellis, Bob Kline, Monte Kahl, Sara Douglas and Judy Stull, thank you for the camaraderie over the years and for making ten grueling hours on the volleyball court seem like a walk in the park.

To all my past and present Lady Cougars of Clinton High School and the USA Junior Olympic Girl's Volleyball players, thank you for playing your hearts out and for the life lessons you have taught me on and off the court. To the Lady Cougar parents, thank you for entrusting your daughters to us for four months out of the year. To Whitey Gilbertson, Bill Greer, Keith Witte, Marci & Becky Korth, and Mark Seymour, thank you for allowing me to be a part of one of the best basketball programs in Wisconsin! (We love you Barb Seymour!) Coach Witte, thank you for volunteering so much of your time to make a difference in the lives of our players. I can't imagine coaching without you.

To the thousands of readers on our HeartTouchers.com and Heart4Teens.com lists: Thank you for being a part of something special as we touch lives across the globe through the power of stories. Your feedback and encouragement played a huge part in getting this book off the ground!

And to my Lord and Savior Jesus Christ for picking Kristi to be my wife, for the gift of my children, for forgiving my sins, changing my heart, and giving me hope for the future!

Sincerely,
Michael T. Powers


To my nieces, nephews, and children: this is my legacy to you. Michael, you and I make a great team! Thanks for being my editor and encourager. And lastly, to Rachel, Shaz, and Christina, for being my kindred-spirit friends. I love you gals!

Sincerely,
Kristi Powers

Special Note:  The photo that appears on the cover is of our son Caleb when he was three years old, which was taken by Kristi while we vacationed in Jekyll Island, Georgia. I knew that it was a special picture when I first viewed it and then later knew that it was the perfect picture to put on the cover of our book.

# Foreword

Professional writers get very irritable when someone informs us that he is planning to write a book "whenever I have the time" or comments that it must be great to "lie around the house, waiting for inspiration." Such folks have no idea how hard writing is, and how often we squeeze assignments in around the demands of another job (to say nothing of a family) or re-think our career choice: on bad days, even elevator repair or medical school seem preferable.

Then, once in awhile, we meet a newcomer ready and eager to master all he can, knowing that the learning will require sacrifice and rejection, who brings to his craft that certain combination of emotion, sincerity and logic and isn't afraid to let it show, who writes because not to write would be worse—and we recognize him. We are us, and now he is us. Such a person is Michael T. Powers.

For the past year I have been enjoying Michael's pieces on his website. They are warm, funny, touching and filled with the family and spiritual values that make him such a solid man. My favorite changes from week to week; sometimes I think he will never surpass "When Lightning Bugs Look Like Fireworks", but then I re-read "Taking Off the Mask" and again, enjoy the goosebumps. How did this young person get to be so good, I wonder? Not just at writing, but at life... People who worry about the moral development of today's twenty- and thirty-somethings ought to read his parenting pieces, his stories of coaching teenage-girl basketball players. They would be truly consoled and encouraged. Fortunately, that's something we can all do. Michael's collection of stories Heart Touchers is finally here. I can recommend it wholeheartedly, and am looking forward to yet another read. Michael, welcome to the "lying around the house" club. May Heart Touchers be only the beginning.

**Joan Wester Anderson**
**New York Times Best-Selling Author of 15 books including**
**Where Angels Walk and Forever Young, the authorized**
**biography of screen legend Loretta Young.**

# Introduction

I started writing in January of 1999 at the ripe old age of thirty. I was talking with my wife, Kristi, one day about something that my son, Caleb, did that was funny, but, for the life of us, we couldn't remember the details. Then and there I vowed to start writing things down about my children. At the time there were about forty family members and friends who were on my e-mail list, and two weeks later I shared with them an experience involving Caleb and our bathtub. A couple of them wrote back, complimented me on my writing, and suggested that I write more. That was all the encouragement I needed! Since then I have written numerous stories and the forty family members and friends have turned into HeartTouchers.com and Heart4Teens.com with thousands of world-wide readers.

I never intended for anything like this to happen, but am truly thankful to the Lord for the way He has worked things out. I write because I want to present my children with a book about their lives when they graduate from high school. I also write because I have to. Something will happen, usually that something will involve my children, and I have to sit down and type. I work two jobs, and have a hard time finding the time to write, but it is amazing how we all make the time for the things we want to do. A story will start building in my head, and I will put it off until I just drop everything and let it come out via the keyboard. Writing has caught me up in its magical flame, and there is a burning inside that demands attention whether I have time for it or not. Writing is also a way to help keep my priorities where they need to be. When I let thousands of people see into my soul, imperfections and all, I feel a huge responsibility to live up to the values and ideals I write about. One theme that is usually constant in my stories is spending time with my children. Since I wrote "The Bathtub Story", I am constantly reminded to make my family not just a priority, but the top priority.

No matter what God has in store for me, I am thankful for the talents He has given me, and I hope to always seek His will in my writing. May I always remember my promise to give my children a book about their lives, a book filled with the magic of childhood, the wonder of learning, and the incredible highs and lows of their teenage years. Most of all, however, I pray it is a book filled with good memories of a mother and father who spent time with their children...

May you enjoy the following stories and may they touch your hearts in a special way.

Michael

# Celebrating Daddyhood

I have experienced many things in my life...

I have coached over a thousand games of softball, basketball, and volleyball; experiencing incredible comebacks, undefeated seasons, a State Championship, and coming one match away from going to the National USA Junior Olympic Girl's Volleyball Championships.

I have felt the incredible elation that comes with playing your heart out for twelve hours on a volleyball court, and then collapsing in your teammates' arms as you win a gold medal at a major tournament.

I have been humbled as I stood at The Wall in Washington DC, running my fingers over its surface; feeling the incredible history, emotion, and power that emanated from the thousands of etched names that represented those who have died for my freedom.

I have been on the mighty Mississippi River and watched the most fantastic sunrise filled with innumerable shades of orange and red, only to have my attention stolen by huge flocks of mallards as they appeared out of the painted mist that slowly rose from the surface of the water.

I have been out in the middle of a snow-blanketed meadow, with the air so cold that it hurt to inhale. But it didn't matter, as my breath was stolen from me as I watched the Northern Lights, or Aurora Borealis as it is known to some. My eyes were transfixed on the velvet curtains of luminescent light as it wavered back and forth across the starry canvas. From emerald green, to cobalt blue, to shades of purple with a hint of crimson, they flowed and danced across the frosty sky. I watched until my entire body was numb from the cold, but couldn't bring myself to look away for fear that they would not be there when I glanced back...

Yes, I have experienced a number of things in my life, but nothing, absolutely nothing, can compare with the joy I feel being a father to my three young boys.

No state championship can compare with hearing my wife tell me that I was going to be a daddy for the first time.

No Gold Medal can compare with hearing the doctor say, "You have a healthy baby boy."

No man-made monument, no matter how powerful, can compare with the first time I saw my son Caleb smile.

Nothing in God's wondrous creation can compare with my eighteen-month-old son Connor saying, "Bless you, Daddy," after I sneeze.

The soft hair on the back of the head of my new infant: Chase. The smell of baby lotion. The squeals of joy when they take their first steps. Seeing the expression of pride and elation on Caleb's face when he caught his first fish. Watching my son Connor bow his head, close his eyes, and "pray" out loud, before he could even talk...

Nothing can compare.

Come experience Daddyhood with me. There is no greater feeling!

"In years past, when I would walk in the door, stressed out and possibly depressed from the dreams in my life that seemed so far out of reach, two words brought me back to what was important in life: 'Daddy's Home!'" —Michael T. Powers

# The Bathtub

The other night I wanted to take a nice hot bath and finish a good book that I had been reading. I was tired and a little stressed, and all I wanted to do was lie in the hottest water I could stand and lose myself in the book's pages. The problem with this little "getaway" for me was the fact that "Aqua Boy" lives in our house in the form of Caleb. There is not a bath that is taken in our neighborhood that he doesn't know about. When he realized what I was going to do, he started asking to take one too. Of course I said no.

"Oh Pleeeeeeeeeeazzzzzzzzzzzze Daddy?"

"Caleb, I said no."

"But I wannnnnaaa!"

After a couple of hundred no's, I told him that I would think about it. Then I put my finger on my cheek and tapped it a bit (to show that I was thinking) and then said no. I probably shouldn't have done this, but hey, we parents can have a little sarcastic fun right? The problem was that Mommy saw me do this. Not good. I know better than to mess with the head of my wife's offspring. Now I knew I was in trouble.

I climbed into the bathtub and turned on the water. Ahhhhhhhh!! This was going to be relaxing...Suddenly there was Caleb. He had asked Kristi if he could take a bath with me after I had read for awhile. She told him to go ask Daddy, so there he was with big old puppy dog eyes that still had tears in them. "Daddy, can I take a bath with you when you are done?"

I knew I was trapped. "OK." I said. "When Daddy is done reading, you can come in here with me."

His eyes lit up and he said, "That'll be great!"

I went back to my book. The next time I looked up he had taken all his clothes off and had plopped himself up on the toilet. He wasn't in a comfortable sitting position either. He had his feet on the seat and he was squatting down like a catcher. I looked at my naked son and asked him, "What are you doing?"

"I'm waiting for you to be done."

"Caleb. When I am done I will call for you and then you can come in. OK?"

"OK, Daddy."

Back to my book.

Once again I heard him come into the bathroom. This time he was carrying his toy fishing pole that he had gotten for Christmas from his Aunt Jana.

"What are you doing, Caleb?"

"I'm just watching you."

"Caleb, you need to leave until I call you."

He pulled up the little stool that he uses to reach the sink to brush his teeth and promptly plopped his naked buttocks down on it.

"Caleb, you can't come in until I am done."

"I know Daddy. I'll just sit here and wait until you are done."

There he sat like Opie from the Andy Griffith Show, with his fishing pole and his really bad hair cut that made his ears stick out...

Back to my book.

In the meantime my wife was sitting out in the kitchen listening to all of this...grinning.

By now it was really hard to concentrate on my book. I had only twenty minutes before I had to get ready for work, and I was really looking forward to relaxing.

I tried to concentrate on the words...

PLOP!

I looked down in the water to see a great big plastic Fisher Price hook... connected to a colorful Fisher Price fishing pole... connected to the little hands of my bare son.

"Caleb. You can't go fishing in the bathtub right now. Daddy is trying to take his bath."

"I'm sorry, I'm sorry, I'm sorry." (Caleb always apologizes in threes.)

Instead of leaving, he remained on his stool. I tried to read, but it was getting harder and harder.

"Caleb. What are you doing now?"

"I'm just gonna sit here and wait for you to get done."

I tried to read one last time, but I couldn't. He sat there next to the bathtub just staring at me with those big brown "doe" eyes, his new fishing pole over his shoulder.

What could I do? He broke me down. Minute by minute he slowly and methodically broke me down and reduced me to emotional mush. My son is not a very patient three-year-old. I guess not many are, but I couldn't believe how patient he was being. He wasn't crying and whining like he usually would in this situation.

My heart went out to him. "Caleb. Do you want to come in the bathtub now?"

"That would be great!" (One of his favorite sayings)

"OK. Come on in."

We had a great twenty minutes of splashing, fishing, and being kids together.

I had wanted so badly to relax and read my book; I had wanted it almost too badly. I nearly missed out on a special time with my boy. When I was driving to work that night, I thought about how many times I have told him no: "I'm too busy..." "Maybe tomorrow..." "Not right now, Caleb. I have a video to edit..."

I'm getting better. I am realizing how special my kids' early years are and how fast they go by. So many times, even when I do take the time to spend with my wife and kids, there is something inside of me which keeps saying, "Do you realize how much time you are taking doing this? Do you know how much video editing you could accomplish right now?"

I'm learning to relax. I'm learning to enjoy my free time. I'm learning to take more free time and, thanks to a wonderfully patient wife and three-year-old, the voice inside me is diminishing to a whisper. Sometimes I can't even hear it. Hopefully, I will block it out totally in the near future. Hopefully that voice will begin to say:

"Michael. Do you realize the investment you are making in your son right now?"

"Do you realize that you are honoring your wife and building a closer relationship?"

"Do you realize that twenty years from now it won't matter that you didn't get that work done as quickly as you wanted?"

"Do you realize that your sons, daughters, and wife have become the most important to you?"

I am a ways off...But Lord willing, that day will come.

# Here's One Last Kiss, Batman

My four-year-old son, Caleb, thinks he's Batman. Not a day goes by that he doesn't put his Batman suit on and try and make the world a safer place for us to live. The adventure began when we bought him a Batman costume for $19.95. It was not the Batman suit of the recent blockbuster movies with its reinforced armor and sleeked-down aerodynamic look. No, this was the kind that Adam West wore in the TV series some thirty years ago. You know, the one where his not-so-athletic belly stuck out and it looked like he was wearing a pair of tights?

Caleb has used it so much that it is torn, stained, and won't even tie around his neck anymore, but the worse the suit has become, the more he has grown to love it. I'm sure that one of our favorite memories years from now will be Caleb throwing his arms and one leg back, pausing dramatically, and then "Whooshing," into the next room, cape billowing out behind him as he fights crime in our Wisconsin home.

While Caleb is Batman, Connor, his one-year-old brother, is Robin, The Boy-Wonder. I don't think Connor likes being Robin, as it usually means being ordered around, but Caleb makes him his sidekick anyway. The Dynamic Duo run around the house letting bad guys know that crime doesn't pay, stopping only to let Connor take drinks from his tippy cup when he gets thirsty. We couldn't find a Robin costume, so Connor has to settle for Caleb's old hand-me-down Superman outfit. Don't anyone dare tell him! He'll figure it out soon enough...

Caleb and his alter ego have become inseparable. Two months ago I took him to a birthday party for one of the high school girls I coach in basketball. My wife was gone for four days, so I took both Caleb and Connor to the party with me. Halfway through the night, Caleb disappeared upstairs for a few minutes. Suddenly, I looked up and there at the top of the stairs stood my offspring with his hands on his hips and a smile on his face. Oh, yeah...and with a very used and abused Batman costume on. He had hidden the suit in his LEGO's bag and smuggled it into the party.

"I'M BATMAN!" he yelled, and then proceeded to run down the stairs to impress the sixteen or so high school girls in the living room below. My players "ooohed" and "aaahhed" at him, and then started giggling. When he got to the bottom of the stairs and turned around, the giggling turned into outright laughter.

"Caleb, could you turn around for Daddy?"

When he turned, I saw right away why the girls had started laughing. The back of his suit was so torn that his naked buttocks were hanging out.

"Caleb, where is your underwear?" I calmly asked.

"I took it off before we left the house, Daddy!" he proudly replied. Then he turned and showed all the girls his bare buns looking just like a patient in the hospital who had forgotten to tie the back of his gown. I didn't know that part of my parental duty was to make sure my children had the proper undergarments on before taking them out into public. Any time my wife leaves me totally in charge of my children, I learn something new.

Caleb didn't like that the girls continued to giggle at him, so he went upstairs to put his regular clothes back on, but five minutes later he returned in his suit and was showing his Bat-Buttocks to the world. Finally, I made him go put his clothes back on before he lost all his dignity, and I my coaching job, for condoning super hero nudity at a team function.

Caleb insisted that we let him take his costume on our recent trip to Florida. While there, we stopped at McDonald's to eat one afternoon so he could frolic on the Playland after lunch. It was a good thing too, because our cuddly Caped-Crusader was needed!

(Suspenseful music)

A little girl was about three levels up on the play tower. Trapped by fright, she was afraid to go all the way up to the top where the slide started, and afraid to go back down the way she had come. The damsel in distress started crying! Her distraught mother was trying to coax her down, first with care and concern, and then by threatening to never take her to the McDonald's Playland again.

"This happens every time I bring you here. I'm never going to bring you here again!"

Suddenly our preschool super hero jumped into action. He scaled the three flights of Playland tunnel-stairs and found the young girl in her perilous predicament.

"Hi! I'm Batman! It's OK! Just follow me up to the slide!"

No response from the stressed-out maiden.

"All right, then! Just follow me down the stairs!"

Still no response.

In fact, she was now staring at our son like he was some kind of a Midwest freak show. Finally, Caleb gave up and climbed back down. I was irreverently thinking, "Of course she didn't respond to you. You don't have your suit on. You can't expect people to recognize you without your suit on!"

The five-year-old girl finally did get the nerve to go all the way up to the slide. I'm guessing she feared a second visit from our budding young hero.

Caleb is constantly bugging me to play Batman. When I am able to, I play along with him. I would like to claim that I only do it because I love my son and want to spend time with him, and most of the time, this is the reason. However, to be totally honest, I was also a four-year-old who loved to play Batman back in the early 70's, and I must admit that I have as much fun as my boy does.

There is one thing I love to do while we play Batman. It doesn't matter what villain I am either. Sometimes I am a traditional bad-guy like the Joker or the Penguin; however, sometimes I am the tickle-monster, and sometimes he just calls me the daddy-monster. Regardless of what bad-guy role I take, there is one "trick" that every villain plays on him. In the middle of the "fight", I throw him down on the waterbed, get on top of him, and then plant about a thousand kisses on his face. The first time I did it, he gave me a look of pure shock. I guess it was the last thing he expected the Joker to do to him. He can deal with punches and kicks; he blocks them or tries to roll out of the way. Pillows sent flying his way can be avoided by ducking...

BUT KISSES!!

Kisses from his arch enemy!? How does Batman deal with that? There is no kiss repellent on his utility belt! After the look of shock passes, another look takes over, a look that could only be described as total and outright BETRAYAL! I am guessing the following thoughts went through his young mind: "Daddy, how could you?! How could you defile something as sacred as playing Batman by kissing me?!"

When I planted the last daddy-monster kiss on his chubby cheek, he just froze, looking up at me with that stunned look on his face, then rolled his eyes at me and screamed, "DAAAAAAADDDDYYYY!!  YOU DON'T GIVE KISSES WHILE YOU ARE PLAYING BATMAN!!

Oh, how I laughed...

He has since become smarter in his dealings with my villainous kisses during our Batman sessions. Now, whenever I start to kiss him, he points to the Batman logo on his chest, and shoots a Bat-ray out of it at me. "I'm turning you back into the Joker, Daddy!"

He figures that these lapses back into daddyhood can be reversed by his special Batman powers. I usually play along with him and immediately switch back to the traditional role of the villain, unless I am especially in the kissy mood.

Sadly, the Batman costume has seen its last days. We will be retiring it very soon, and most likely replacing it with a new one. In fact, we may look for the suit that is based after the Batman movies of today and hopefully it will be better-made this time. However, when we do, I will be taking the old, ripped-up, stained, and worn-out suit, and will be setting it aside in a special place—the special place reserved for magical childhood memories...and for things to show his first girlfriend. (Hee hee).

While I realize that these precious times with my children are flowing through my cupped hands like water, I know that in the future I will take the suit out from time to time, to try and recapture the early years of my kids' lives. When I am done reminiscing, I will place the suit back in its hiding place, but not before rubbing the wetness from my eyes. I am determined that the tears that appear there will be drops of happy remembrance, and not of regret, wishing I had spent more time with my children.

Here's one last kiss, Batman...

*****

Snow, snow go away for little Caleb wants to play.
'Cause digging in the dirt is fun, but can't be done without the sun.
The ground is hard and will not yield to hands or shovels in the field.
In winter there's no bugs to find so thoughts of Spring are on his mind.

# The New Father Fog

Kristi has been extremely creative in how she tells me I am going to be a father. When she knew she was pregnant with our first son, Caleb, she took me to a nice restaurant for dinner. At the end of our delicious meal, the waitress handed me the bill and a sealed envelope. She told me it was from someone in the restaurant. I looked around, searching for a familiar face, but found none. I opened it and read the typed message. In the meantime, all the employees, including the chefs from the kitchen, started moving closer to our table.

The message read, "Michael, this is to inform you that you will be changing the kitty litter for the next nine months. In other words, congratulations, you are going to be a father!"

I looked across the table at my beloved wife with disbelief on my face. "How did this happen!" flashed through my head. I remembered the talk my father had with me long ago, so I knew how it happened, but I wanted to know HOW this had happened! I started bawling like a baby. I had wanted to have children all seven years of our marriage, but Kristi wanted to wait. This was not something we had planned, and I wasn't emotionally ready for it. There I sat, tears streaming down my face, surrounded by my now crying wife, a bunch of sobbing waitresses, and a couple of chefs who went back into the kitchen in a suspicious hurry.

The next eight months were filled with anticipation and moments of wonder. I remember hearing the sound of my baby's heartbeat. Nothing prepares a man for the moment he hears his child's heartbeat for the first time. It was nothing like I expected. The chugging that came through the speakers sounded just like a train to me. I know that doesn't sound too exciting or romantic, but to me it was incredible.

I remember watching my wife's tummy grow, longing for the day when I would be able to feel Caleb moving inside of her. We would sit for long periods of time, my hands pressed gently against her abdomen, waiting for Caleb to move, but he wouldn't. I would pray that God would give him the hiccups just so I could feel my son through the thin layer that protected him from the outside world.

And then miraculously he moved and I felt him for the first time! I waited breathlessly for him to move again, not believing that it actually happened. I can't even imagine what it must have felt like for Kristi to sense her offspring moving within her.

As I waited for the day of his birth, I would have dreams of seeing him for the first time; intensely vivid dreams of a baby's face that would stay with me long after sleep ended.

Looking back now, I am amazed at how long, and how short, nine months can be.

We never did get to rush off to the hospital like on TV because Caleb decided he liked it too much inside the womb. After being three weeks overdue, the doctors decided to induce labor, so there we sat in the hospital waiting for something to happen. Kristi wanted a CD player in the room so she could listen to relaxing music as she went through the huffing, puffing, and pushing. I, however, thought it would be funny to put in a CD by Salt-N-Peppa and play their song, "Push It," so as soon as I was sufficiently bored with waiting, I turned the CD player on and out blasted: "PUSH IT! PUSH IT GOOD!"

I was so proud of my little joke.

When I looked up, I saw Kristi and her mom giving me the death stare. Not even a crack of a smile. I was grinning from ear to ear, but realized that if I wanted to be a part of this miracle and stay in the room, I had better turn it off in a hurry and put on some soothing music. To this day they don't think it was funny, while I am still laughing out loud as I write this. In their defense, Kristi tells me that the music was so loud that they couldn't make out the words.

Labor finally set in—twenty hours of it. At the end of the twenty hours, Caleb's head was too big for the birth canal, and the doctor told us he would have to do a C-Section. At this point I was a little worried, but trusted that God and the doctors knew what they were doing.

Then it finally happened! I was sitting at the head of the operating table, holding Kristi's hand, when the doctor said, "We have a healthy baby boy." All throughout surgery, I was afraid to stand up so that I could see what was going on. I figured the doctors and nurses would yell at me and say, "Boy, what do you think you are doing?! You sit back down now!" However, when I heard the doctor say that he could see the baby, I didn't care if they threw a scalpel at me; I was going to look at my child.

There he was! I could almost hear the angels singing as my precious baby boy was brought into the world. He was perfect in every way, and the tears began to fall.

"Oh Kristi! He's beautiful!" was all I could stammer.

I was in the "new father fog."

In reality, Caleb looked terrible. His skin color changed about four times in the first five minutes, and I wouldn't have been surprised to be on the cover of the National Enquirer: "Reptile Boy Born in Wisconsin! Man fathers chameleon in real life X-Files episode!" His hands and feet were extremely wrinkled, like he had been in the pool too long, and all kinds of bodily secretions were oozing from his pores.

Everything else seemed fine, though... Except for THE TWO HEADS!

Yes, my boy had two heads, and that was the first thing Kristi noticed when the nurse handed Caleb to her for the first time. She told me later that she was thoroughly convinced that she had married a psycho. "My husband called this thing beautiful?"

Because Caleb went through twenty hours of labor, but had been too big to fit through the birth canal, it was obvious where his head had been stuck all that time. It had swollen up like a balloon in two different places, and it really did look like he had two heads. Being the proud father, I figured that was God's way of storing all the brain matter he inherited from me. The swelling did go down in a few days, but Caleb wasn't looking his best for the first few weeks.

It is amazing, though, how being a new father blinded me to certain realities. I kept telling everyone how beautiful he was. It wasn't until a year or so later, after looking at the video, that I realized Caleb had looked like a swollen two-headed lizard that had been in the water for too long. To me though, he was the most beautiful creation that had ever appeared on the earth.

Fatherhood. You gotta love it!

# Tuxedo Swimming

This past week I took my three-year-old, Caleb, to his first swimming lessons at the local YMCA. I had been looking forward to some father/son bonding time ever since my wife had suggested doing this earlier in the year. The day before, I asked Kristi to call the YMCA to find out what we were supposed to bring, what time we were to be there, and any other important details. I work third shift and have a hard time making calls during the day when I'm sleeping, so I just wanted to make sure I knew what I was getting into.

We left half an hour early, just to make sure we were there on time, and went to the locker room to change. We got our swimsuits on, put the rest of our clothes in a gym bag, and proceeded to make our way out through the showers and into the pool area. I was really looking forward to this. Me, my boy, nothing on but our swimsuits, and a pool full of water. What could be better?

Well, I rounded the corner, holding hands with my excited son, and an inaudible gasp of horror escaped me. There in the hall next to the pool were ten to fifteen parents and their young children. All the children had their swimsuits on, but every one of the parents were fully dressed. Let me rephrase that...All the mothers were fully dressed. There was not another father to be seen for miles. I WAS THE ONLY GUY!! Some mothers were in dresses and power suits as if they had just come from the office, while others wore jeans and shirts. But the important thing was, THEY WERE ALL FULLY DRESSED!!

I could just hear what they were thinking:

"Who is the three-year-old with the hair on his chest?"

"Can a man really have a chest that goes into his body instead of out?"

"I thought you had to be a corpse to have skin that white?"

"My sunglasses! Where are my sunglasses?! OH THE HUMANITY!"

"He must have tapeworms. Something has to be stealing his nourishment."

"All this weight equipment at the YMCA and he still looks like that!"

I wanted to scream back at them:
"I TRIED LIFTING WEIGHTS BUT THEY'RE TOO HEAVY!!"
I wanted to crawl into a hole and hide, but there was nowhere to go.

The nice young high school girls who were teaching the swim class started explaining that the parents were to stay out in the hall and watch their kids through the large windows. The only time they were to go near the pool was if their child was crying or misbehaving. Otherwise the teachers didn't want the children distracted by their parents while they were taught not to drown.

I slowly reached into my gym bag and pulled out my T-shirt. Trying my best to be cool and nonchalant, I was able to cover the top half of my body, and, by the time she was done talking, I was fully clothed.

Caleb had a great time as I watched through the windows and tried to avoid any possible conversation with another human being.

When I came home, the first thing out of Kristi's mouth was, "How come you're not wet?"

After I explained what had transpired, she laughed and laughed until her stomach hurt.

For some reason, even after the phone call, we were both under the impression that I would get to frolic in the water too. The best part of the whole story is: I have to go back and face these people again today at 4:30, and twice a week for the next month or so.

I think I might rent a tux for today's swimming lesson.

*****

## Caleb Short Take

One night at the dinner table Caleb looked at his plate and said, "I'm full."

I told him, "Caleb, you haven't hardly eaten anything off your plate."

"Ohhhhhhh..." then he sighed and said, "I always say that when I just want to get up and go play."

"Caleb, that's called lying," I replied.

"But Dad, it's just a little lie."

"Caleb, a lie is a lie. You need to tell the truth."
"Awwww dad. I just can't seem to get the hang of it!"

# When Lightning Bugs Look Like Fireworks

On the Fourth of July, Kristi and I went a couple blocks from our house to a huge hill where we could enjoy the view and the fireworks, not only from the town we live in, but from nearby towns as well. It was a hot night, but there was a wonderful breeze, and we could see a long way in all directions.

I wanted to see our three-year-old Caleb's reaction to the fireworks. He sat with us all of two minutes before he started tumbling down the hill and giggling.

"Caleb, come here."

He would reluctantly come back by us and sit for a spell.

"See the pretty colors over there?"

"OOOOOhhhhhhhh!" he replied, all the while looking in a different direction from where the fireworks were actually going off.

"Heeee heeeee!" he giggled as he tumbled down the steep hill again...

"Caleb, come here and watch with Daddy."

"OK, Dad."

Back up the hill he would come. I tried getting him to concentrate on the fireworks again.

He watched for another twenty seconds before he started walking away from us.

Suddenly he let out a squeal of delight. "Finally, he is enjoying the fireworks," I thought. He yelled out, "Look at all the lightning bugs!"

I sighed and looked down the hill; indeed, there were literally hundreds of fireflies that were stealing Daddy's thunder.

I tried in vain one last time to get him to watch with me. "Caleb, tell me what colors you see."

"That's a green one, Daddy! And a red one!"

This lasted another minute or so before he reached in the stroller to tickle Connor, his eleven-month-old brother. Then he was off tumbling down the hill again, saying, "Whoa, whoa, whoa, whoa," with each spin of his body. I started to call out to him again when Kristi leaned over to me and whispered, "Michael, just let him be a kid. There will be other years."

I had been getting so irritated that he wouldn't sit by us and take in the fireworks. I guess I had this preconceived notion that he would sit on my lap and just squeal with delight every time one exploded. Then he was going to ask me if they were magic, so that his proud Daddy could stick out his chest, and explain away. Luckily my understanding wife was there, and was able to gently nudge me back to reality.

There was nothing wrong with my expectations, but once again my impatience was getting in the way of enjoying time with my wife and sons. I should have picked up on the cues and tumbled down the hill with my boy. Fireworks have been around for hundreds of years, but my boy was only going to be three years old for another week.

I bet when a person tumbles down the hill, the lightning bugs look like fireworks going off. I guess I'll have to start a new tradition on the Fourth of July. Actually, from what my three-year-old tells me, the show goes on every night!

*****

**Long Live Raffi!**

Parents of young kids know that as soon as they get into the car, the Raffi tape, or some other kid's song collection, has to be played. Sometimes it is fun to sing along with my kids, and sometimes it can become a great big headache!

One day, while driving to the town of Clinton for basketball practice, I found myself singing along with one of Caleb's tapes: "Down on Grandpa's farm there is a big brown cow. The cow she makes a sound like this: MOOOOOOO, the cow she makes a sound like this: MOOOOOOO. Oh, we're on the way, we're on the way, on the way to grandpa's farm!"

I sang and "mooed" for twenty-five straight minutes. As I pulled into the parking lot at the high school and turned off the engine, I realized that my two young boys were safe at home with Kristi, and that I had sung Raffi songs the whole trip for no reason other than the tape started playing when I started the car and I was used to doing it!

# True Strength

Father's Day has come and gone and I have been thinking a lot about what being a father means the past couple of weeks. The question I have asked myself is: When does the son take on the father role? At the age of thirty-one, I still view myself as a teenager bumbling my way through life, not knowing how to handle certain situations.

As a young boy growing up, I always looked at my father as someone who had all the answers... someone who knew what to do in all situations... someone who never worried or doubted his decisions... someone who could fix a toy, take a splinter out of my finger, or repair a car.

I never thought that my father might have his doubts. In fact, if I would have know this growing up, I might not have felt as secure as I did in my childhood.

Now that I am a father to Caleb and Connor, I am the one who "knows all the answers, and is sure of himself at all times." Hah! Now that's a good one! But guess what? That is how Caleb and Connor view me. It was like a flash of lightning struck my consciousness. My father had the same doubts and concerns that I have now. He didn't show it, and I didn't know it.

There have been many times when I didn't have an answer, but I remember one incident especially, a time when the cold wave of despair washed over me. It was a few weeks before my second son, Connor, was born, and something came up that I had no idea how to handle. Exactly what happened is a story for another time, but know that it was most likely the hardest thing I have ever had to deal with in my life. I was faced with the possibility that I might never be able to work the problem out.

I can't even begin to describe how it felt.

Yes, I can. I felt as if my head had been slammed face first into an ice-cold brick wall—repeatedly. It felt as if a huge boulder had been placed on my chest, and a serrated butcher knife was being slowly twisted into my back. Oh, yeah, there was the burning bile that rose in my throat, and the feeling that I might vomit at any time.

Years of dealing with this problem had come to a head: all the doubts and fears that I wasn't doing the right thing... all the times I wept bitterly over what to do... all the prayers asking God and mentors in my life for help and guidance... and even the times I asked God why? Why, God? Why did this have to happen?

It all came crashing over me in one huge tidal wave and I lost it. My wife called work and told them I wouldn't be in that night, and I went down in the basement into my video production room and collapsed in a heap. I wept as I have never wept before. I cried for nearly half an hour as I poured my heart out to God seeking answers.

It was then that I heard a soft voice at the door. "Daddy? You OK?" The door slowly opened and there stood Caleb, who was about a month shy of his third birthday. I didn't know what to do. Do I let my boy see me like this? Do I shove the hurt and pain down inside and hide my feelings? I tried, but I couldn't. A fresh wave of sorrow billowed over me as I struggled with my indecision.

Caleb walked slowly over to me and sat down on the floor next to me. I tried so hard to be "strong" and not let him see me like this, but, try as I might, I couldn't stop crying. He slowly reached his chubby little hand up and started stroking my cheek. "It's OK, Daddy. It's OK."

My heart wanted to burst.

"Don't cry, Daddy. It's OK."

I grabbed my son and hugged him close to my chest and we sat there and rocked on the floor for the longest time. Then he looked up at me and said, "Love you Daddy. I'm going to go play with my animals now."

I kissed his rosy little cheek and out the door he went.

That night was a turning point for me. The unnamed problem is still there, but I know now that I have done everything that I could possibly do to rectify it. I have totally given it over to my heavenly Father, who does have all the answers.

Now, as I go through my daily life, I realize that I am not going to have all the answers, or even the questions, for that matter. I will be strong when I need to be, and I will be a solid foundation for my kids to build their lives on through the help of my Lord and Savior Jesus Christ. I will always remember the day when my three-year-old son lent me his strength through his touch and his simple words. The day I realized that being strong sometimes means showing my weakness.

"My grace is sufficient for thee: for my strength is made perfect in weakness."

2 Corinthians 12:9

\*\*\*\*\*

**Connor Short Take**

I came into the kitchen the other day to hear my five-year-old Connor talking to himself. He was saying:

"Dad. Dead. Dead. Dad." Repeating those words over and over. He looked up at me when I entered the room.

"Connor, what were you saying?" I curiously asked him, hoping that I had not walked in on the secret plotting of a young assassin.

"I was saying, Dad. Dead. Dead. Dad."

"Hmmm..." I said in morbid curiosity. But before I could say anything else, Connor continued.

"Isn't that amazing how much those words sound alike Dad?" Connor blurted out with a giggle.

"Yep! That is pretty amazing, Connor," I sighed as I walked back out of the room, thinking about sending my kids to public schools where they don't teach about alliteration until they are much older...Homeschooling was making them think too much in their spare time.

# Vomiting and Other Parental Delights!

I was told to call home from work this past Monday night at about 3:20 a.m. My heart sank, as generally a "good" call at work doesn't happen at that time of the morning. I was pretty sure my wife didn't wake up in the middle of the night with an overpowering urge to call me and tell me she loved me. (Although, it could happen!) I prayed quickly and said, "Lord, please let everyone be OK."

When I returned the call, my wife answered the phone and told me right away there was nothing wrong with the kids. She went on to tell me that she made some cookie dough and decided she should eat some before she baked it. Well, she ended up releasing the contents of her stomach at least a couple of times that night and things were going from bad to worse. She guessed she might have food poisoning from the raw eggs in the cookie dough.

I hurried home to help her take care of the kids in case she had to go to the hospital. She slowly, but surely, got better as the day went on.

Then Wednesday came.

I was getting ready to go to basketball practice when Kristi asked if it would be possible to take Caleb with me. (We had a surprise birthday party to go to after practice for one of my players.) A couple of times during practice my son told me that his tummy didn't feel well, but two minutes later he was running around laughing and trying to get himself killed by dashing out on the practice floor and dodging out of the way of players running full speed down the court. (But, hey, if you are a guy what better way to get killed than to be trampled to death by a bunch of athletic women?!)

Now if I were a mom, I would have known right away that something was up with Caleb. Besides the tummy complaint, he was being a little more whiney than usual, but I thought that maybe he was just tired. How could he be sick if he was still laughing and playing? When I am sick, I let the whole world know it, and I mope around and let myself be babied by Kristi.

We all piled into a couple of vehicles and headed over to Megan Stevens' house for her surprise party.

Warning number two: If Caleb doesn't want to eat fruit, things aren't going well. Megan's mom, Melanie had a wonderful layout of fruits and veggies with dip to tide us over until the pasta was done. Caleb didn't want any of it. Then he was offered some Chex mix with M & M's!

"No, I don't want any." Caleb replied.

(HELLO, MICHAEL! Are you paying attention to the warning signs?! Caleb just refused candy! Get out of the house now!!)

Kristi then called me from home to check on how Caleb was doing. She told me that Connor, our five-month-old was throwing up. I told her that Caleb had complained about his tummy so she advised me that I should probably not spend too much time there after everyone ate. Caleb came up to me shortly after and wanted me to hold him so I picked up my boy and held him close...

He softly said my name and looked up at me. His eyes glazed over for a second, then a look of terrible fear passed over his countenance. (For you Green Bay Packer fans, that means his face.) Suddenly there was food and stomach bile everywhere. I detected the faint aroma of All Sport, and remembered that Caleb had some of that just before we left practice. He vomited all over me, himself, the floor, and the wall. After about the third wave, it suddenly occurred to me that I should be making my way to the bathroom. After about twenty seconds of running blindly through the house, I realized I had no idea where the bathroom was! Megan finally caught up to us and guided us into the bathroom, but not before he threw up once more in the hallway. It is one thing to vomit at our own house, but quite another to defile someone else's domain.

There we were in the bathroom, soaked to the skin in partially digested food and grape-flavored All Sport. Normally I would have freaked out. I am the type of person who can't stand having anything like that come into contact with my skin. If my five-month-old spits up on me, I act like the stuff is acid and have to get it off of me immediately! If my kid has a runny nose, I have to wipe it off right away. In this case, however, all I could do was laugh. What a party to remember!

One of our basketball players, Rebecca Ligman, or "Barka" as everyone calls her, is very susceptible to the sight of blood and many other wonderful functions of the human body. I thought for sure that she was going to start a chain of eruptions and that the whole birthday party would be one big scene from the movie "The Exorcist." I was very proud of her, though, as she left the grisly scene to compose herself, then came back in to be a big help to us, along with the birthday girl, Megan, and her mom, Melanie. In no time Melanie had her pristine country style house looking good again, and Megan and Barka had us in new T-shirts. Barka even grabbed our nasty shirts and put them in a plastic bag for us to take home. I was so grateful to everyone. I realize that these things happen, but if I am in my own house, it is easier to handle. Who cares if you vomit on your own walls and floor. But just try doing it at someone else's house and see how you feel?

Not once did I feel like I needed to be ashamed for what happened. Melanie just went into "Mother Mode" and took care of everything...I was thankful to everyone there for not being too grossed out, and for making us feel comfortable.

We left as soon as we could, and then started the race to try and get home before the next emptying began. We made it home in time. When we walked in the door, I saw that Connor was just lying on Kristi's stomach. He could hardly hold his head up. Then he started throwing up. What a heart-wrenching sight to see. Here is this little baby, usually all full of energy, just lying there like he is dead, and then convulsing and trying to empty his stomach. I felt so helpless.

Caleb broke my depression by telling my wife, "Mommy, I throwed up poop at the girl's party!"

The night continued on with both kids getting sick a couple of more times, and Daddy getting a dose of parenting reality.

Mommy went to bed early as she was still recovering herself, and I was faced with the responsibility of holding down the household all by myself with no help from her. You see, most of my time with the kids is play-time, eating meals, and the many other fun things involved in parenting. I don't do much of the down-and-dirty parenting that my wife usually does. Boy, do I appreciate her a lot more after that night and the next morning.

Parenting is a lot of fun. I enjoy all the wrestling, snowball fights, and tickling, but I have a new appreciation for my wife and the parenting that she does in the trenches. It's one thing to be responsible when the good times are rolling, but yet another when you are cleaning up vomit, staying up late with a sick child, or even cleaning up after an accident in the bed when a three-year-old has the flu. Taking care of children when one is tired, feeling sick, or just plain stressed out is a lot of work and takes tremendous patience, but it is something that my wife does extremely well.

I just told her to never get sick again!

# Word Of Mouth

A customer whom I was helping put together a video about her husband's life was at our house recently. After four to five hours in my video studio in the basement, she asked to use the bathroom before she went home. She went upstairs and asked where the bathroom was, and was greeted by our helpful three-year-old. Caleb showed her where the facilities were and came running excitedly out to Kristi, my wife, in the living room.

"MOMMY! I SHOWED DADDY'S PRISONER WHERE OUR BATHROOM WAS!"

Kristi just about choked on what she was eating...She glanced nervously at the bathroom door.

"Daddy's prisoner? You mean the lady Daddy is helping?"

"YEAH! DADDY'S PRISONER!"

"Caleb, she's not a prisoner."

"BUT THAT IS WHAT YOU AND DADDY CALL HER!"

I was still downstairs and didn't realize that my boy was scaring my business away.

In the meantime, this poor unfortunate soul is sitting in our bathroom, which is only a couple of feet from our loud and excited three-year-old, probably thinking, "Please, Lord, let me get out of this house alive!" I could imagine her trying the window latches in the bathroom to see if there was another way out of the house.

Finally, Kristi caught on to what Caleb was getting at.

"You mean Daddy's customer, right," Kristi asked, all the while praying that she was on the right track, before a frantic person ran screaming and yelling out of our house, half-dressed, and dragging a roll of toilet paper behind her! (Not the best form of advertising for my growing business).

"YEAH THAT'S IT! DADDY'S CUSTOMER!"

Cindy walked out of the bathroom and left our house without showing so much as a hint of fear. We later found out that she had heard, and was amused by, the whole thing as we have been fortunate enough to get to know her better since then. She's on my e-mail list now, and she even scheduled another appointment to come back and finish her video project.

I guess word of mouth is the best form of advertising even if the words come from a confused three-year-old.


\*\*\*\*\*


**Caleb Short Take**


The other day our three-year-old Caleb, used his Fisher Price three wheeler in the house. He didn't ride it; he used it as a stool to climb up on the counter, and then he began looking through the cupboard for something to eat. At this time Michael found him standing there and lectured him on not climbing up on the counter and how some day he was going to come crashing down on his head and hurt himself so badly that his brains would come gushing out (Michael, like Caleb, has a flair for the dramatic). In all seriousness, Caleb looked at him and said, "And then I will have to go see Jesus." I just happened to be walking into the kitchen at that time and quickly backed out...laughing all the way.

# This Life That Lies Before Me

I wanted to introduce everyone to my little sister, Christina Miller. Other than being the most fertile in the family, (she has five kids under the age of seven!) she is a stay-at-home-mom, singer, and songwriter. She is the type of person who wakes up in the middle of the night and has to find a pen and a piece of paper. Why, you ask? Because the words to a song have just come to her and she wants to write them down. Her husband, Jeff, besides being an engineer, is also a talented singer, guitar player, and songwriter. The two of them have talent just oozing from their pores. I envy them both. I know that I shouldn't, as I am beyond thankful for the talents and gifts the Lord has given me, but just once I would like to sit down and just make up a song—or better yet, go to sleep and have the words to a song just scream out that they need to be written down!

When we had Caleb dedicated to the Lord three years ago, Jeff and Christina attended the service along with other family and friends. After the pastor and congregation prayed for Caleb's young life, we went back to our seats, but to our surprise, Jeff and Christina walked up to the stage. As they smiled at us, Jeff took out his guitar, and Christina pulled the microphone close to her...They had written the words and music to a song just for Caleb, and had asked our pastor if they could sing it to us at the dedication. Try to imagine what went through my mind after my first born son had been dedicated to the Lord, and my sister and brother-in-law, whom I dearly love, sang the following words to us:

**This Life That Lies Before Me**

As I unwrap this precious gift, this life that lies before me
I cannot fathom what you will give, this life that lies before me
So with faithful and earnest prayers, we lift him to you, Father

With open hearts and open hands, to protect him through life's troubled
waters
And we ask...

That Your hand of peace be upon him
That Your eyes of love will too
That Your mercy ever surround him
No matter what we do
Yes, that Your hand of peace be upon him
That Your loving eyes will too
That Your mercy always surround him
That Your protection be about him
And that his life would be forever
Dedicated to You.

I don't remember what life was like without him
And I cannot imagine my life without You
For such perfect and precious gifts could only come
From the One whose gifts are true

So, I unwrap this precious gift, this life that lies before me
And I will give all that I can give to this life that lies before me
The many smiles and all the trials in this life that lies before me
Will be lifted high to his Father and Friend, oh this life that lies before me
And we ask...

That Your hand of peace be upon us
That Your eyes of love will too
That Your mercy ever surround us
No matter what we do
That Your hand of peace be upon us
That Your loving eyes will too
That Your mercy always surround us
That Your protection be about us
And that our lives would be forever
That our lives would be forever
Dedicated to You

Copyright 1995 by Christina Miller (Tinifer@yahoo.com)

I cried all the way through the song. Not only did it make me think of the precious life that God had given to us through our first son, Caleb, but it reminded me how much I loved my sister. It was one of the best "gifts" that we have ever received in our lives, and we are so thankful to Jeff and Christina for the love they showed us that day.

\*\*\*\*\*

**Connor Short Take**

While we enjoy the myriad of wildlife on our camping trips, including wolves, bald eagles, whitetail deer, grouse, turkeys, coyotes, red fox, black bears, turtles, frogs, raccoons, and other small fur-bearers, (notice I did not include skunks, but that is another story!) we especially enjoy watching and listening to the loons. One of our favorite camping memories is of little toddler Connor and the loons that live on Bear Lake. Kristi and I were sitting around the campfire our first night of Connor's first camping trip when the loons began their hauntingly beautiful cry. It echoed across the lake and through the north woods. Then, from out of the tent, where we thought Connor was sleeping, came the loon's answer. Connor, who was eleven-months-old at the time, did an uncanny loon imitation. For the next twenty minutes or so, Kristi and I held hands by the fire and listened to nature's loon talk to our little loon. For the rest of the week it became a nightly ritual...

# A "New" Hero is Born

The other night a new superhero appeared in our house! As most of you know, my two little boys love superheroes, and I have written a couple stories about their exploits as Batman, etc.

Every Wednesday night we have the teenagers of our youth group over for a small group Bible study. Soon after the bible study was over, and while teenagers were still hanging in our living room talking to one another, I was surprised by a speeding blur that came down the hall! The tan colored flash of movement came to an abrupt halt in the middle of our crowded living room.

"I AM NAKED MAN!" shouted Connor, my five-year-old son, as he stood there in all of his natural glory.

Then with a whoosh he was heading back for the safety of his room.

Teenage laughter bellowed out along with an exasperated "CONNOR RICHARD POWERS!" in stereo sound as my wife and I both called out to him from opposite sides of the house.

As most of you parents know, I was faced with a dilemma. I was roaring with laughter inside at the sight of my new little superhero, but I also had to make sure that my five-year-old knew that public nudity was not an acceptable practice here in Wisconsin.

I made my way into the "Buff Cave" where Naked Man hung out in his spare time.

"Connor." I said in the most menacing parental voice I could muster.

"Yes, Daddy," replied Naked man as he tried to pretend he was sorry for what he just did, but the twinkle in his eye told me otherwise.

"Connor, you know better than to run out in the living room without your clothes on," I scolded him.

"I know..." he sighed as looked down at the floor. Then he looked up at me and said, "But that sure was pretty funny, huh, Daddy?"

I busted out laughing. Then Naked Man started laughing. Then I realized I was supposed to be teaching him a lesson. I cut off my laughter in mid giggle.

"Yes, that was pretty funny, Connor, but you are never going to do that again, are you?

"I know Daddy," the UnCaped Crusader replied hanging his head.

"Now get some clothes on you little cutie patootie!"

I kissed his naked forehead and made my way out the door, all the while listening to Naked Man's giggles, and him saying to himself, "That sure was funny!" as he put his clothes back on...

Yes...a "Nude" hero was born.

I couldn't wait until all the students left, our two little boys went to bed, and it was just my wife and I alone in the house.

Connor had given me an idea...

*****

## Caleb and Connor Short Take

I have some strange children...which shouldn't surprise me, considering who their father is. As we were driving in the car, I looked in the rearview mirror to see them playing tag. Yes, my 5-year-old and my two-year-old were playing tag in the car. Now that might not seem too unusual to you, but consider that Connor was in his car seat, and Caleb was exactly two inches away from him, with his seatbelt on.

"Tag! You're it!" shouted Connor after he smacked Caleb on the back.

"Tag! You're it!" shouted Caleb as he tagged Connor back.

Each would turn their bodies, as if to run, every time they tagged one another. Ah yes...my future Valedictorians are off to a good start.

# Celebrating Sports

I love sports and all that they teach us...

They are not about all-star teams, wins and losses, conference titles, or state championships. Don't get me wrong. Those are honorable goals to set, and if a team didn't have them, I would question its motive. No, sports are about the journey. They are about the camaraderie that a team feels over a season and the incredible feeling of accomplishment when players have worked so hard on something and finally see the fruits of their labor. They are about the melding together of different backgrounds and personalities into a "team"— into a family. As with siblings, disagreements take place, but when it is time to go to war on the court, they come together and play as one entity. Players who outwardly hate each other before a season starts, can learn to respect and sometimes even admire each other over the course of a season.

Sports are about the look of tentative confidence on a young lady's face when she finally starts to believe in herself and her teammates.

They are about the triumphant grin on a player's face when she hits the first three-pointer of her career.

They are about the starters who stand and cheer wildly from the bench for those players who have taken their place on the court. They are about team huddles, high fives, hugs, pasta parties, trips to Chuck-E-Cheeses, and white elephant gifts at Christmas time.

They are about laughter, tears, sweat, and sometimes blood. They are about highs, lows, discipline, hard work, and self-confidence.

They are about leaving skin on the floor, purple badges of honor that appear on knees, and feeling like emptying one's stomach after putting every part of one's being on display to a gym full of people. They are about the euphoria a player gets when their team battles all night and their competitors hurl everything in their arsenal at them, but they come together and stand strong, with a common purpose and goal.

As sports columnist Mark Whicker stated: "Sports is life with the volume up. The friendships in sports are fused more tightly than in most places. The laughter is louder, the jokes funnier, the pain sharper, the nights later, the lows lower. Athletics teach us that life, although unpredictable, is something we can deal with. A team nods when it wins and shrugs when it loses and wakes up to a new and different game each day."

Sports teach us that we are not alone, and that by working together we can do something special.

In other words, sports are about life...

# The Day Lisa Lost

I admire athletes!  Don't get me wrong. I'm not talking about the many professional athletes of today who have developed a "me-first" attitude, after being raised in a "win-at-all-cost" generation, where role models are severely lacking, and too many of the headlines that capture our attention are of those athletes who are in trouble. No, I am talking about high school sports, where lessons of life are still being learned, and where athletes still compete for the love of the game and their teammates.

I know some of you are thinking: "The high school athletes of today are just as bad," and you would be partially right. The "me-first" attitude is trickling down into the high school and junior high athletes.

In the midst of all of this, however, is a young lady from Wisconsin.

I first met Lisa Kincaid on the volleyball court as she played for a rival conference high school. Many times I was on the opposing sidelines as a coach, and could only watch in awe at her athleticism:  the speed of a cheetah, the mental toughness of a veteran, and a 32-inch vertical jump! She possessed skills unheard of for a high school girl—and she was only a sophomore!

Starting her junior year, I was fortunate enough to coach Lisa on a USA Junior Olympic Volleyball team, and it was during these two years that my wife and I grew to love and respect her, not only for her many athletic achievements, but for her unselfishness and humility toward those around her in the face of the many honors that were bestowed upon her. Besides being one of the most coachable athletes I have ever had, she was the epitome of a team player and went out of her way to be humble.

If anyone had a right to be cocky or proud of herself, it was Lisa. Besides being one of the best volleyball and basketball players in the state, she became a track legend. How good was she?  She went sixty-four straight conference meets and never lost in any event she entered. She made trips to the state finals all four years she was in high school, and came away with six state titles. Many times she was her team's lone representative at the state competition, and would single-handedly place her high school as high as third. While she excelled in the triple jump, long jump, 100- and 200-meter dashes, there were times when her coach needed her to fill in for other events. One particular day he asked her to run the 300-M hurdles. She had never competed in this event before, but the coach needed her that day for the good of the team. How did she do? She not only won, she set the school record in the first and only time she competed in that event!

Never once did she ever brag about her accomplishments. In fact she felt uncomfortable talking about her achievements and would usually steer the conversation away from herself and to the performances of her younger sisters or other teammates. Besides coaching her in volleyball, I was able to see her at many track meets, as I was hired to produce track videos by other high schools in the conference for my video production company. I saw many instances where she would loan her shoes to someone who forgot them, or slow down at the end of a race to finish up stride for stride with her sister, both of them smiling from ear to ear as they crossed the finish line together. Also, I vividly remember Lisa going up to an athlete from a different team and wishing her a happy birthday. The young lady's face just beamed as she told Lisa of her birthday plans for later that night. I was smiling as I walked away, because I happened to know that it was Lisa's birthday that day, too, but never once did she mention it.

However, there was one particular track meet during Lisa's junior year that she impressed upon me what is still good about sports these days.

It was a non-conference meet late in the year and Lisa's coach entered her in the 1600-meter race. Lisa had never competed in this event before and was puzzled as to why she had been entered.

Lisa easily outdistanced the competition, but on the last lap, she "seemed" to grow "tired." Two athletes from the other team passed her, and then so did "Jane," Lisa's teammate. Lisa stayed just behind her teammate and crossed the finish line at her heels...

Lisa "lost" an event for the first time in her track career.

You see, athletes in Lisa's track program needed to earn a set number of points in order to earn a varsity letter. Lisa knew that Jane, who was a senior, needed to finish at least third to earn a letter for the first time. Lisa also knew that the two athletes on the other team were most likely going to beat Jane if they ran anywhere near the times they had been running all year, but that, barring an injury during the race, Jane was a lock to finish third. That was until the coach entered Lisa in the event.

Lisa remembered all this as she lined up for the start of that race, and I wondered why she had a slight smile on her face after having lost for the first time ever, until I figured out the rest of the story.

After four years of working hard, Jane finally received her first varsity letter, and helped her team win the meet. And Lisa? On that day, she earned my respect and admiration, and in my mind, she solidified herself as the role model this generation sorely needs.

"Sometimes you can lose and still win."

*****

## Caleb Short Take

I asked Kristi if she would make me a bowl of cereal the other day. She was in a hurry and heading out the door and told me she didn't have time. Caleb, my oldest boy, came into the kitchen, looked at me, put his hands on his hips, rolled his eyes and said:

"Daddy, I'm six years old, and I make my own cereal every day. What did we do? Switch brains or something!"

From now on, I will be making my own cereal.

# Common Bond

Ladies,

Saturday night you will play for the Wisconsin State Championship in girl's basketball, and it is the culmination of four months of hard work. Millions of girl's basketball players never get the opportunity to play for a state championship in their high school careers. You get that chance. You get that chance because you have earned it; you get that chance because you have worked your behinds off all year, and now you play to prove something to yourselves, to your teammates, and to the opposition...

Four months ago 128 teams started out with a dream to become Division 3 State Champions...and now it comes down to two teams. Four months of five-woman weave, Wisconsin Drills, sprints, ball handling, more sprints, scrimmaging, three-on-two-two-on-one, box out games, shooting drills, and lifting weights. Four months of playing your hearts out in games and practices and now that dream comes down to thirty-two minutes.

Make every second count. Make every touch of the ball the most important of the game. Every time a shot goes up, box out the opposition and rip down the rebound. When you see a loose ball, dive head first, arms and hands extended, without even thinking of what may happen to the skin on your knees. If you think you have played hard on defense this year, think again! Oh yes, we have played stellar defense, but it is nowhere near how hard we are going to play this next game! Tell yourself to play defense with your feet, and with the most important muscle in the game of basketball —YOUR HEART! When you throw your heart into the game, your body will follow.

When you step to the free throw line, the crowd noise fades away and you visualize the two swishes that will be taking place. You say to yourself, "What were they thinking when they fouled me?! Don't they know that I never miss!?" And then you see the swish in your mind. You feel the smoothness of the ball as you release the most perfect shot, with the most beautiful backspin. It rises ever so slowly to the peak of its arc, and then drops smoothly through the net... and all of this happens in your head before you even receive the ball from the ref.

I can feel the energy building within you already. Each and every pasta party has contributed the carbohydrates, and somewhere, deep down inside your reserves, there is a ball of flame that is just waiting to explode. All it will take is just one of you, just one player who decides to set herself on fire. When the rest of you brush up against that player, you burst into flame also! This flame will be so bright that our legions of fans will have to look away for a moment or go blind. The student section will pull out their sunglasses as they sit in the stands and bask in the glow that is the Lady Cougars...

You know what is going to make the difference? Confidence! Confidence is the cement that binds a team together. Confidence is contagious. Confidence is intimidating. From the time we step foot into the Kohl Center, they will see the look of confidence on our faces, and the other team will know the game is over before it even starts. The Lady Cougars have years and years of tradition behind them. We are winners. It is what we do.

However, being a winner is much, much more than just outscoring another team. You ladies are winners because you love and respect your teammates and coaches. You are winners because you have come together as a family, through the good times and the bad, through the wins and the losses, the pasta parties and the team talks, through the easy games and the games where we sent players to the emergency room. You are winners because you beat teams by playing tough basketball and not by playing dirty. You say "thank you" to the refs each time they hand you the ball and you look the other team in the eyes, shake their hands, and mean it when you tell them they played a good game. When the other team elbows you in the ribs, or shoves you to the floor, you don't fight back. Instead you calmly walk to the line, sink both free throws, and then slyly look at the scoreboard where you have just inflicted "your" damage. You are winners because you study hard in school and realize that playing basketball is a privilege that can be taken away at any time. You are winners because you have made a commitment to each other, and to the coaches, to spend four months of your young life stuck in a smelly gym, sweating like an animal, when you have hundreds of other things that are calling for your time.

You are winners because you are Lady Cougars: Amanda, Ami, Aundrea, Brittany, Chrissy, Diedra, Hannah, Kim, Jacqueline, Kayla, Kelsey, Nancy, Sam, Sarah, Stacey, and Tina. Powerful names by themselves, but a monumental force to be reckoned with when you join hands and come together as a team.

May all of you know how much we love being your coaches and how much we love being a part of the incredible Lady Cougar tradition. Walk off the floor Saturday night knowing that you played your hearts out, and that you left every ounce of hustle and every drop of sweat on the court behind you. Hold nothing back. Walk off the court with your heads held high, as "The Champions" we know you are, no matter what the scoreboard says. In basketball, and more importantly in life, all of you are winners in our books.

Thank you for a magical season...

I love ya!
Coach Powers
P.S. I leave you with a song that my sister Christina wrote for the Lady Cougars:

## COMMON BOND

We are friends and we'll stick to the end.
We are friends for all time.
We are friends and we'll stick to the end.
'Cause there's something we all share inside.

It's a common bond and it runs through our souls.
A common bond that helps us to grow.
It's a common bond that I hope you will see
A common bond always flowing through me.

No matter what we do, we do it with strength.
No matter where we go, we go with power.

No matter how we play, we play with thanks
To the common bond that gives us strength.

There's a magic in our fingers and power in our stride,
There's a confidence that only comes from the common bond inside.
When the sky is at our feet and the globe is in our hands,
I'll remember the common bond that has made me who I am.

It's a common bond and it runs through our souls.
A common bond that helps us to grow.
It's a common bond that I hope you will see
He's always flowing through me.
He's always flowing through me.

Copyright by Christina Miller (Tinifer@yahoo.com)

End Note: The Lady Cougars of Clinton, Wisconsin did indeed win their first State Championship over Thorp by a score of 57-44. Congratulations Ladies! The 2003 Division 3 Wisconsin State Champions!

*****

**Caleb Short Take**

One day when Caleb was three, he looked up at me and said in his long and drawn out fashion, "Daddddy, when I grooowww up, I want to be a girrrlll, so I can play BASKETBALL!!"
I had to explain to him that boys play basketball, too, but I guess three years of coming to the girls' practices at Clinton High School have made an impression on him.

# What Really Matters

It was the second game of the year for our basketball team. We had just played the night before and destroyed a team by a wide margin. This night we were playing a much larger school but we were very confident that we could beat them.

As a coach, I was looking forward to this game. Beating another school by more than thirty points is nice, but it really doesn't help us as a team. Facing a team that we know can beat us if we don't play at the top of our game is what competition is all about. Taking our small school team into their home gym and fighting it out with them toe to toe is the type of challenge I relish.

There was one other person who was really looking forward to this game, and her name was Karen Van Nevel. Karen was ill the first game of the year, and didn't get to play, but this night she was ready, as there weren't many things that Karen looked forward to more than the basketball season. After working incredibly hard all summer and fall, she had improved herself in every area of her game and had earned a starting spot on a team that was loaded with talent.

The ref threw the ball in the air and the war was on.

Halfway through the game, our manager, Christin Ingolia or "Iggy" as she is nicknamed, taught me something about loyalty as she was videotaping for us on the other side of the court. The other team's fans starting making fun of me, particularly the way I was dressed, since I like to dress-up for coaching. I feel that a coach sets the tone for his team, and when I am in jeans, I don't command respect, so most of the time I wear a suit. This particular night, I had my best one on. Iggy was videotaping right in front of their bleachers and she heard them talking about me.

"Who does this coach think he is wearing a suit to the game?"

"Hey Tie-guy! Your team is going to lose!"

Iggy was standing there looking calm, but inside her blood was beginning to boil. Finally, she had had enough. She turned around, planted her fists on her hips, and scolded them all.

"HIS NAME IS NOT TIE-GUY! (Dramatic pause)   HIS NAME IS MR. POWERS!"

Then she calmly turned around and continued capturing the images of the game on video.

When my wife told me what had transpired, it warmed my heart. You see, Iggy tried out for the team at the beginning of the year, but we had to cut three people and she was one of them. I remember telling the players that we would be making cuts at the end of practice, and I watched her as she made her way out of the locker room and across the gym floor. I dreaded this moment. I have never had to cut anyone before in my eleven years of coaching three different sports, and I wasn't looking forward to it. She tried not to make eye contact with me, and I had to call out and ask her to come and see me. I could see in her eyes that she knew what was going to take place.

When I told her the unpleasant news, the tears just welled up in her big brown eyes. I told her we would love to have her around as a manager if she wanted to. She walked away with tears streaming down her cheeks, and I didn't think she was interested in ever seeing my face again.

To my surprise she showed up the next day and asked to be a manager for the team, and we were glad to have her. It made me take a step back and realize just how lucky I have been to have always had classy kids in our program. To have her defend me like that meant the world to me.

Back to the game...

It was an intense and physical game from the start and neither team was going to back down. The game itself was a classic battle, and had everything that a good high school game has to offer, but I won't go into it in depth. Just know that the game was tied at regulation, and we went into overtime.

With forty-five seconds left in overtime, we were up by two points and I was feeling confident. Our defense was playing well, and the other team was frustrated. While trying to set their offense up for one last play, one of their guards launched a three-pointer from way behind the three-point line. As the shot left her hand I could hear the other coach yell, "NOOOOOOOOOOO!"

It was not the shot they wanted. I caught my breath as the shot arched gracefully through the air. The wind went out of me as it swished through the net. Now they led by one point, and there were only twenty seconds left on the clock. We passed the ball up to half court and called time out.

After the time out, we were working the ball around looking for a good shot, when the ball ended up in the hands of one of our star players. Unfortunately, she bobbled the pass when she caught it, and it slipped out of her hands and bounced off the floor. She picked it back up.

"Don't dribble!" I yelled.

Now the clock was counting down. 7-6-5...She got flustered and dribbled the ball to make a move to the basket. The shrill whistle of the ref cut through the air and he called out, "Double Dribble!"

I felt so bad for her. All the other team had to do was inbound the ball and the game was won. They did so, and dribbled up the floor at full speed. I took my eyes off the court, as I knew the game was over, and I glanced up at the scoreboard as the horn sounded to end the game. The horn never really ended as the most blood-curdling scream I have ever heard split the air. There was Karen, who had played her heart out all game, writhing in agony on the floor. She went to plant her foot on the sideline to take a charge just before the buzzer sounded and something in her knee tore loose.

Time seemed to freeze for everyone, but her screaming did not. The crowd grew totally silent and the celebration of the other team ended prematurely. Her next scream jolted me into action. I sprang off the bench and ran to Karen only to find that Kim Gilbank had beaten me there. How she got there before me, I'll never know, as she was on the bench with me at the time. Karen kept screaming, "COACH!!!!   IT HURTS SO BAD!!!!!"

I knelt down and grabbed her hand. A sick feeling started in my stomach and began to flow through the rest of my body as I realized that she had done some major damage to her knee. In all my years of coaching, I have never had an athlete sustain a serious injury on the court. Kim and I both offered what comfort we could, as someone went to call her parents. Karen was squeezing my hand so tightly that it left marks for minutes afterwards.  I looked across from me at Kim, as she held Karen's other hand.  The salty drops were flowing freely from her eyes now as she was there for her "bestest friend."

The loss of the game was a thing of the past. The intense struggle to prove who was the better team seemed so insignificant, as I looked down into the agony in her eyes. I also saw the terrible disappointment as Karen knew in her heart that this was the first and last game she was going to play this year. I glanced up and saw that the rest of the team were now all huddled around us. Almost everyone had tears in their eyes as they struggled with the helpless feeling that came over them as their teammate rolled on the floor in horrid pain. Tears would be expected after the hard fought loss, but now there were tears of concern as they gathered around to support their teammate. Kim told her buddy that she loved her as her tears dripped down onto Karen's face. I felt so helpless as all I could do was try and comfort her through the pain. I tried to take her mind off the agony with some humor, but each laugh that she started ended with a moan. Coaches and parents finally carried Karen out to the parking lot, where Kim and her folks took her to the emergency room.

Karen had surgery and was told that it was the worst sports related knee injury that the surgeon had ever seen.

I did a lot of reflecting after that game. We put so much emphasis on things which, in the whole scheme of life, are really unimportant—like winning or being better than another team. Who really cares if you can put this orange sphere through a metal ring better than the next person can?! I am not just talking sports here; it could be anything that we put our time and energy into, like the big job promotion, the new car that we just have to have, the hobby that we are consumed with, or any number of things that we so carefully plan. Plans change as life throws things our way.

In the midst of intense competition I found myself learning things that I didn't expect to learn on a basketball court. I learned about family, loyalty, true friendship, and being there for people when they need help.

At our end-of-the-year banquet, I can assure you that the most important thing that I will talk about is not going to be the eighteen or nineteen games we will end up winning. No, it is going to be the game that we lost—the game when we all learned what was really important in life.

# Heroes Among Us

I have a challenge for you. Do you have a hero in your life? I want you to take a few moments and write about him or her. Yes, that means you have to stretch your fingers out and do some typing or better yet, make it a hand-written note. When you are done, send it to your hero. That simple act will not only make that person's day, but it will also be your way of thanking them for all they do in your life.

To start the ball rolling, I thought I would share a letter that I wrote to my hero. Everyone knows that my wife is my hero, but there is someone else who has been my hero since sixth grade, when I moved from the suburbs of Chicago, Illinois to the small town of Clinton, Wisconsin.

Here is a letter I sent out to Bill Greer this past winter. He is someone who has had a tremendous positive impact in my life as a teacher and coach, and now as someone I coach with at Clinton High School.

Dear Bill,

You have been and always will be a role model for me and literally thousands of students and players who have been influenced by you as a teacher and a coach. From the first day I met you when we moved here in the sixth grade, I have watched you, copied you, and taken many of life's lessons from you. While I only had you for a coach one time when you subbed for baseball, I have watched, listened, and "stolen" coaching methods, ideas, and mannerisms from you. My whole coaching style and philosophy is 75% Bill Greer, 20% Mike Wesling, and 5% everyone else.

My respect for coaches was incredible when I first started coaching in 1989. I was totally overwhelmed when I realized the tremendous "POWER" that coaches have to influence a student's life for good or for bad. It was almost too much for me when I realized how I could totally destroy a player's self-confidence by uttering a single word, or even by giving the wrong facial expression at times. I remember praying and asking for help so that I would always keep the players and what was really important in their lives first, and then worry about wins and losses second. One of the coaching quotes that has always meant a lot to me and has always reminded me of you is:

"Coaching is to create the best person we can out of the athletes we meet. Our secondary goal is to make them the best athlete we can."

My goal for any team has always been that the players can look back on their year and say to themselves, "Those were some good times." If a team has a great year record-wise, then that is a bonus. Ten years from now not many people are going to remember who won the conference, or which team went to state, but if they built relationships with each other that lasted, felt like they accomplished something personally, and can look back and laugh about the fun they had, then I feel like I have done my job as a coach. That is something that you have done remarkably well. Besides having an incredible win-loss record in every sport you have taken on, you have taught so many "life lessons" that have affected players for the rest of their lives. My wife has story after story of things you did when she had you as a coach. It seems to me that the things she remembers most are those that had little to do with basketball and everything to do with life. Athletes play their hearts out for Coach Greer, not because they fear him, but because they don't want to disappoint him. When athletes play out of fear, or to show up a coach, their whole heart is not in it, but when an athlete plays hard for herself and because she doesn't want to disappoint a coach, then she is playing with her whole being. When that coach continues to build confidence, she begins to play hard not only for herself, but also for her teammates.

I respect you most for that.

I have heard many a player reflect those same thoughts about you. When I first started coaching at Clinton High School, I was intimidated out of my mind. I will always remember my second practice. We were scrimmaging your team, and you were the only one who was talking, teaching, and coaching. I was too afraid to say anything in front of you for fear that I would be wrong. You pulled me aside and said, "You know, Mike, you can start saying things to your players anytime now. Just relax and be yourself." The legend had given me permission to talk, and it was okay to do so!

I have a long way to go as far as basketball knowledge is concerned, but I have been learning that, and what is most important in life, from you. Thank you for who you are, what you stand for, and for being someone I have always looked up to. I look forward to the future, except for that sad day when you decide to hang up the whistle for the last time. I hope and pray that day is far from now, but wanted you to know that you have touched so many lives that anytime you walk away from the game, you can hold your head up high and be proud for being willing to let the Lord use you in so many ways.

Besides my dad when I was growing up, you have always been the man I most respect and admire in life.

Very Sincerely,
  Michael

Who is your hero? Take some time this week and write to him or her. You never know, it might make all the difference in the world to hear from you!

*****

**Caleb Short Take**

I was taking Kristi and the boys to O'Hare airport one morning so they could fly to warm, sunny Florida to visit Grandma. I, on the other hand, had to stay in Wisconsin where it was bitter cold. Caleb, the actor, decided it was time to go for an Oscar nomination. Just before they left on their plane he said, "Daddy", sniff, sniff, (He then gave me a big hug and stepped back from me) "Daddy, I sure hope I miss you!" Then he proceeded to pretend to try to make himself cry.

# For the Love of the Game!

Hello there, sports fans!

This past weekend's volleyball tournament is a prime example of why I love sports!

The tournament we played in was a Reverse Coed 4's tournament, which means the net is set at women's height (7 ft. 4 in.) as compared to coed or men's height of eight feet. The teams consist of two males and two females, but the men can't hit or block the ball at the net. In other words, males who want to hit the ball must jump from a line that is ten feet behind the net. The relatively new format is very popular and is geared toward making the men play defense and set, while the women pound away on a net height they are more familiar with. Believe me, trying to dig a ball hit by a National All-American on a women's height net is downright scary!

My team consists of Mary Jaskolski or "Jazz" as we call her, Dee Horn, Jay Potter, and myself. We all have roles to play. Dee and Jazz pound the ball, Jay sets, and I run around and make sure the ball never hits the ground. It is a pretty good arrangement and we all do our jobs well. (I always surround myself with players who are better than I am, and that is one of the reasons my teams have been so successful in the sport.)

One of the things I love about the volleyball culture is all the "talk" that goes on. Before we had even arrived at the tournament, my team was supposedly not even a team. Four or five people walked up to me and said, "What are you doing here? I heard you were too sick to play" Then someone else told me that it was too bad that Dee hurt her knee and couldn't play. This was news to me, and I was worried about not even having a team to compete with. Well, Dee showed up and told me about her knee, but she said she was playing no matter what.

This particular tournament had twenty teams from all over Wisconsin and Illinois, with a few players from other neighboring states. We look forward to this tournament every year, especially since it is a money tournament, and we had won the last three years in a row.

This particular year, however, we knew we had a tough hill to climb. From the start, we had two strikes against us. Dee's doctor had told her she had a torn meniscus in her knee the Wednesday before the tournament. I had bronchitis and was told to stay in bed for three days, hadn't played in a tournament since the summer, and had tried to find someone to sub for me, but couldn't get anyone. Jazz had not played in months, either.

Those who play volleyball know that it is not a sport players can take off for a period of time, and expect to play well when they touch a ball again. We should have been smart enough to stay home, but it was 8:30 in the morning, this was the Winterfest Tournament, and we wanted to win.

The twenty teams are broken down into pools of five. Each team plays two games a piece against the other four and the top two teams from each pool advance to the playoffs. We made it out of pool play by finishing second and we were seeded fifth coming into the playoffs. One team beat us both games earlier in the day, and, while we had been defeated in a single game before, we had never had a team beat us both games until this year. Right away doubts started to set in. I know that I was worried. We found out later that this particular team went around telling everyone, "Yeah, we just beat the team that won the tournament the last three years...They weren't that tough!"

By now we had played eight games of volleyball, and it was 3:30 in the afternoon. Dee's knee was getting sorer as the day went on, and it was getting extremely hard for her to warm up again in between matches. For an all-day tournament like this, we play for an hour straight and then may have a half hour or longer in-between each match where we get stiff and sore, but now it was playoff time. As soon as a team loses in the playoffs, they go home. For a player, everything leading up to now was just coasting...Now the real fun began. I was just hoping we had enough energy to make it through what was ahead. I felt like I was half-dead, and Dee was having a very tough time with the pain in her knee.

I started to wonder if this was all going to be worth it. We had had so much success in the past that sometimes I take for granted what it takes to play at a high level. I wasn't really into it at the time.

Just before the match started, I saw that Jillian Lucas, her dad, Chuck, and Megan Stevens walked into the gym. Oh no...Here were two players who loved volleyball, but whom I also coached in basketball. I knew I was in trouble. I preach to my players that they should always give 100% and that anything they hold back has been lost forever. I thought, "I don't know if I can do that right now." It had been so hard to get myself pumped up and in the right frame of mind, but they single-handedly put my mind and body into gear because I was so afraid of losing in front of them.

Our first playoff match was going to be extremely tough. It could very well have been a match-up for the finals, and neither of our teams wanted to play each other so early on in the playoffs, as one of us was going to get knocked out. Our team got into our little huddle before the match started, looked each other in the eyes, and knew without saying, "IT WAS TIME TO GO TO WORK!!"

Well, we won the first game 15-11, but the second game was a different story. They started beating us, and, before we knew it, we had lost 10-15. At this point I had been throwing my body around recklessly, and I didn't know how much I had left in me to give. Now the momentum had switched, and volleyball is such a game of momentum. What I love about sports is that it mirrors life so well. The mental game of volleyball had kicked into high gear, and each one of us was fighting our own little mini battles in our heads. "Are we going to be able to pull this out?...Maybe this just isn't our year...Even if we win this one, we still have two more matches to play. Maybe we should just go home now?" All these things go through players' heads, as they fight to keep a mental edge, and to persuade themselves to keep fighting. The thrill of competition had swept me up in its intoxicating grasp, and there were two things that were keeping me going. One was Dee and the incredible determination she had to play through the pain, and the other was my fear of losing in front of my players.

The third game was close all the way up to about 8-8. At this point we started to make a run. When we are on a roll, we like getting the ball back in a hurry after the point so we can keep a good thing going. We scored a couple of points in a row, and then the other team started purposely trying to slow down the game. They would walk to get the ball and then roll it sloooowwwllly back to us. Jazz went back to serve again, called out the score, and served. The other team just caught the ball. "We weren't ready," they said. Right then and there I knew we had this game won. Why? Because no one messes with Jazz. Jazz is the type of player that needs something to fire her up, and, boy, oh boy, this was what she needed. Many times the thought has crossed my mind to tell Jazz that the other team had just insulted her mom, or some other outrageous thing, even if they hadn't, because I know that is all it would take to get her fired up.

Two plays later, one of the women on the other team got into it with Jazz about something else, and I was just grinning inside.

"HELLO!!! YOU ARE JUST GETTING JAZZ MAD AND NOW YOU ARE GOING TO PAY FOR IT!!"

Jay and I knew at that point that all we had to do was sit back and watch the fireworks. Dee had already been playing like a woman possessed, and now we knew we had both of our star players into the game. (In fact, Jazz was a two-time National All-American Volleyball player in college.) We trounced them—didn't even let them score another point. With each point I could feel our grasp on victory get tighter and tighter. With each point, we yelled louder and louder. With each point, we put another nail in their coffin until they had no hope and their sad little heads just hung in despair. (Sorry. Got carried away there.)

At game point we were so focused and together as a team, we knew we could not be stopped. It was an incredible feeling. This is what I love about competition—the coming together with a single goal and purpose, and the feeling that no one can stop us. Every time we dove for a ball we could hear the crowd murmur, and with every long rally, we could hear them cheer. I loved every second of it.

One team down, two more to go.

Now the hard part came—the waiting while we got stiff and sore, and the incredible mental letdown as the adrenaline started to subside in our systems.

My two players who had come to watch went home, but I knew that I couldn't face them the next day without winning the tournament. Dee disappeared for a while, and I really started worrying about her. She had been taking medication for the pain, and I could tell she was having trouble moving.

Our next match was against a team that hadn't lost a single game all day. They were seeded first coming out of pool play, and we knew that, although this was considered the semifinals, we were in for another battle that could easily have been a finals match-up.

It took us much longer to get loose this time and Dee was obviously limping. We promptly fell behind 7-1. At that point, because of time constraints, all games were only going to be to eleven instead of fifteen points. Once again the doubts starting creeping in...It is amazing to me the incredible battles that go on in a person's mind, oblivious to what is actually taking place on the court. If an athlete can overcome the mental stuff, the actual physical play is secondary sometimes.

Even though all of us were having our doubts, we never showed it to each other. One of us would do something that would show the other three that he or she wasn't giving up, and then the rest of us would feed off of it. We made a run and tied the game at seven, but, before we knew it, we had lost 11-7. We were in trouble. The hardest thing to do in a best-of-three match is to lose the first game and come back to win the next two. In fact, we had joked with the team before the match and said that whoever won had to do it in two games. No third game! Now that we had lost the first one, how easy would it be to just give in? (When the tournament was over, we admitted to each other that we were all wondering if the streak would end here, but nobody verbalized it at the time.) We got in our huddle and said, "OK, we get to do this the hard way. We might as well play three!"

We scored the first couple of points, and then we began to feed off each other again. One of us would make some spectacular play and then yell out, "WE ARE NOT LOSING!!" Each play brought us closer to the frenzy that makes us so successful. By now all four of us were cramping up at times. More than once Dee would go down hard, and just scream on the floor, and she wouldn't get up for a few seconds. Every time I thought, "That's it. She just ripped her knee up," but every time she would get back up with a smile on her face, and say that she was just mad that she hadn't blocked that ball, or whatever. Later on we found out that she was cramping up and didn't want to show it. Every time I dove for a ball, my calf muscles would bind up in an incredibly tight ball, and there were times when my shoulder would cramp just from the continual shrugging of the shoulders when I passed the ball. Each one of us starting cramping, but the others didn't know it until after the day was over because we didn't want to quit. We got the momentum going and just rolled over them 11-1. At this point, we were afraid to stop playing for fear our bodies wouldn't respond. Our bodies were telling us it was time to stop, and I can honestly say that it felt like we had given everything, including our reserves, but we still had a game and a whole other match to play.

We all grabbed our Gator Aid, refueled, and walked back on the court. Of course the third game wasn't going to be easy, and it went right down to the wire and somehow we pulled it out 12-10.

So many times during this game I thought it was over. I didn't know how we were going to keep the high level of effort going. I kept thinking, "It's OK to lose, Michael. You are sick, Dee is hurting, and Jay and Jazz don't have much to give anymore. If you lose, you get to go home and rest..." But all I could think was, "My teammates aren't giving up, and, if they can gut it out, so can I. I am not facing those girls tomorrow and telling them that we lost."

I have very vivid memories of what took place. My body was screaming to go home. We had just given everything we had, as if it was the last match of the day. Each one of us wanted to go home right then and there. I could see it in the eyes of my teammates. In fact, we even discussed splitting the first and second place prize money with the other team and not playing the finals. Of course, we were just joking...Or were we? I bet if the other team would have come up to us and offered that, we might have taken it. To each other, we weren't going to admit it, however, and we said instead that we should combine the money and play for all or nothing.

Dee had a tremendously hard time getting loose for this one and she was in total pain after her first warm-up hit, but she just smiled and said, "I'll be ready."

We decided to do it the hard way again. We lost the first game of the match. By then we really thought it was over...The team we were playing in the finals just happened to be the team that had beaten us earlier in pool play. Now they had beaten us three straight games.

This was the same team that had been going around telling everyone earlier in the day that we weren't so tough to beat. It was at this time that Jay decided to tell us what they had been saying to everyone all day. Now it was personal. Now it was redemption time. It was now or never! I kept thinking, "Jay, why did you wait until now to tell me this! I needed this motivation in the first game!" Oh, well, now we had the "Us Vs Them" attitude. This attitude does wonders for a team. It's where we decide that the whole world is against us and only my teammates and me can come together to stop it...(Athletes sure are weird, aren't they?) We had a rough start and the score stood at 4-7.

All they needed was four more points and they would win the tournament and would have beaten us four straight games. Things weren't looking good. I had all but given up when I finally realized what I was doing. I couldn't believe that I had let doubt creep into my thought process, and I was ashamed that I let it happen. As a coach I would never let my players give up, no matter what the score was, or how many times a team had beaten us in the past. Here were my teammates working their butts off, and I was mentally giving up! Once again we started feeding off each other. When one of us wanted to give up, the others would refuse to let it happen. It was an incredible thing to be a part of. I am always positive, always confident, always the leader that refuses to lose, but when I started questioning if we could do it, Jazz, Jay, and Dee just got fired up and started screaming how we were "gonna win," and they weren't going home until we did. It got me fired up again, and we started playing hard.

We climbed back in the game one painful point after the other and pulled out the victory.

In the third game, though, we struggled again. It was now after 8:30 p.m. and we had been playing since 8:30 that morning. The score was 5-8 when we called a timeout. We looked at each other, clasped hands, and vowed that we weren't going home without the prize money. We came out of the timeout and willed ourselves into the game. By this time there was almost no one left in the gym watching us play. Now it was purely pride. Now it was, who wanted it more, who had more desire, who would be the last one standing? We scored a couple of quick points and we started gaining momentum. Another point, and I stopped feeling the cramps. Another point, and we started screaming to anyone left in the gym, "WE WILL NOT BE DENIED!!"

We literally whipped ourselves into an adrenaline-filled frenzy that just snowballed after each point. Once again I felt as if nothing could stop us, that it was futile for mere mortals to try to beat us, and that we had better win in a hurry before I fell down and couldn't get back up!

The last three points went by so fast! It was as if the whole match was, at first in slow motion, and then, all of a sudden, someone hit the fast-forward button. Blam, blam, blam, the last three points were ours, and we were jumping around, screaming and hollering, and then we just collapsed in each other's sweaty arms and almost cried when we won. I have never felt more satisfied after a volleyball tournament in my life. The incredible desire to win that came from my team just gave me tingles. I knew then and there why I loved sports so much. I learn so much about myself, and what I am capable of doing if I want it badly enough. I learn to depend on my teammates, and I realize that I can't do it without their help.

I know some of you may be reading this and thinking, "Michael, you have totally lost it! Why would anyone go through what you four did for a stupid game?" For me it was an incredible feeling. I can't begin to describe the feeling of taking all the physical pain and stress and combining it with the mental ups and downs of the day, and knowing that it was all worth it in the end. We walked away with a fourth straight title, a closeness to each other that we had never before achieved, a greater understanding of what it means to rely on our teammates, really sore and sick bodies, and $400 to make us feel better. Oh, yeah, and some really cool T-shirts.

And you know what? All four of us would do it again in a heartbeat!

Are we freaks or what?

"Winning is best defined as earning the respect of your opponents, and the love of your teammates."

\*\*\*\*\*

**Caleb Short Take**

Kristi and I were talking one day, and Caleb kept asking us to stop so he could talk to us. We told him that when other people were talking, he needed to be patient and wait until they were done before he said something to them. He has had a hard time with this concept, so we figured we needed to stick with it. We told him he would have to wait but he continued trying to interrupt us, so we kept talking. Finally, he put his little hands over his ears, stomped his foot and yelled, "MY EARS ARE TIRED OF YOU GUYS TALKING!" We abruptly stopped talking, looked at each other and laughed, and then grabbed him and gave him a big old hug.

# Celebrating Relationships

I have often dreamed of a log cabin up in the mountains away from civilization. Me sitting in a chair by a fireplace, just writing away... But as wonderful as that might sound to a writer, I believe that I would grow restless after a while due to my need for contact and interaction with people. The need to love and be loved, to laugh and cry with others, and to form tighter bonds with those I care for in my life.

I am learning to listen more, to ask sincere questions, and to let other people know that I care about them. And I have found that the best way to do this is to get them talking about themselves. When I close my mouth and really listen, the bonds of love may start out as silk strands, but eventually strengthen into steel cables – unbreakable steel cables that stand the test of time.

However, my biggest problem is that I spend so much time cultivating relationships with those I coach, work with, or play volleyball with, that I let slide the ones that matter most: the relationships with my wife and kids. Ask any of my players and they will say that they know I care about them. But ask my wife that on any given day, and you might be surprised at her answer.

Developing and cultivating relationships, especially with those you are really close to, is a tremendous amount of work. Like anything in life that we care about, they take maintenance and one simple key:  TIME.

Take the time to cultivate the relationships in your life...

# You Don't Get Engaged by a Creek!

As a young boy in eighth grade, I vividly remember praying to God to bring a Christian girlfriend into my life. I didn't have to wait long before the matchmaking that God had planned even before I was born was put into effect.

It was November of my freshman year at Clinton High School, and a gorgeous looking senior girl by the name of Kristi Conway stopped me in the hall. I had the name Powers on the back of my shirt, and she asked me if I was John Powers' brother. I stammered, "Yes I am..."

"Do you think you could give me his address at college so I could write him?"

"I would be more than happy to do that," I croaked.

I was love struck. A senior girl had actually talked to me. What am I saying? A female of any grade had just talked to me, and I was on Clouds Nine, Ten, and Eleven!

Later that day I was in the gym shooting baskets with a teammate until basketball practice officially started. Coming out of the girls' locker room was the woman of my dreams. Her team had just finished up with basketball practice, and she was heading home for the night. Here was the perfect woman, the woman who had talked to me earlier in the day. So what if she wanted my brother's address? She had talked to me...and now she was looking at me...and she was smiling, not just any smile, but one that lit up the whole gym and made my heart beat faster. I couldn't take my eyes off her as she seemingly glided in slow motion the entire length of the court making her way to the hallway door. I was in love, and all was well with the world.

Suddenly I felt as if I had been stuck with Cupid's arrow. And it hurt! I couldn't believe that Cupid had such poor aim and had shot me in the head, because now there was an intense pain in my cranium and the ground rose sharply up to meet me. The sound of a certain senior girl's laughter rang in my ears as she exited the gym.

My teammate, my buddy of all people, had thrown the ball to me while I was staring at my future wife. The ball had hit me in the head, knocked me off my feet, and I lay there as three wavering images of Kristi walked out the door. I figured the relationship had ended before it even started, but the situation proved to be a good conversation starter the next time I saw her.

I never thought the friendship between Kristi and I would turn into a boyfriend/girlfriend relationship. We started out writing letters back and forth in study hall. When we found out we were both Born Again Christians, we had common ground for discussions. All the while I knew this was the woman for me, but knew that because she was a senior and I was a freshman, she would be going off to college and that would be the end of it. I prepared myself for that to happen.

I grew to love her for her kindness. I have yet to meet a kinder, more compassionate person. She was always putting other people first. Students would come to see her about their problems, and she became their unofficial counselor. When I talked to her, it was as if I were the most important person in the world to her. Our friendship grew through letter upon letter and three-hour phone conversations. I will always remember the first time I spent more than an hour talking on the phone to her. I had always thought that people who talked on the phone for more than two minutes were dorks with no lives. My entire life up to this point was filled with phone conversations like:

"Hey Mike, you want to play baseball today?"

"I'm there dude!" Click.

I remember smiling to myself one night after I hung up and looked at the clock. I had just spent more than an hour talking to a girl on the phone! I finally understood why people spent hours on the phone.

During the rest of the school year we grew closer together as friends, and friendship blossomed into something more as we wrote hundreds of letters that we still have in a drawer today...like the letter I wrote to her urging her to find someone else. Why? Because I had crooked teeth at the time. "You are so special, Kristi. You deserve someone with good teeth..." and the letter went on and on as a fourteen-year-old poured out his greatest fear to the woman he loved. How could she stay with me knowing I had crooked teeth? She assured me that she loved me and hadn't even noticed my teeth. She thought the letter was so sweet that she showed it to one of her best friends, Beth Mignon. I was mortified when I found that out.

AAAAAHHHHHHHHHH!! She showed my letter to one of her friends!!

However, I got over it. As scary and frightening as that was to me, when it was the woman I loved, I would forgive her for anything!

I remember the first time we held hands. We were sitting on the couch at my house watching TV with my little brother and sister. I don't remember how our hands got stuck together, but man, oh, man, the fireworks were going off overhead! I was actually holding her hand! But then, my heart stopped. Out of the corner of my eye I saw my dad walking towards us! What do I do?! If I let go of her hand, it might draw attention to it and he might see it! If I didn't let go, he was bound to see us anyway! I could hear the theme from the movie "Jaws" as he moved closer and closer...

Dun, dun. Dun, dun. Dun, dun. DUN DUN DUN DUN DUN DUN!!

I quit breathing. He walked into the room, grabbed something from the shelf, and walked out without so much as saying a word to us.

(EXHALE)

It was right about this time that I remembered a prayer uttered by a lonely eighth grader. This time my prayer was different. "Thank you, Lord, for bringing my Kristi into my life." I had forgotten to thank God for answering my heartfelt prayer as an eighth grader.

Six months after we started going out, I kissed her for the first time. She went to kiss me on the cheek and I turned my lips to her before she knew what was happening. My God-given athletic ability was proving to be useful as my quickness stunned her and she went ahead and kissed me on the lips!

The heavens opened, a shaft of light came down from the sky, and a host of angelic voices sang, "Hallelujah! Hallelujah! Hallelujah!"

Our lifelong love was sealed with our first kiss. When my head stopped swimming, all I could think to say was: (Are you ready for this?)

"So, how was I?"

I had never kissed a girl before, since she was my first and only girlfriend. Why had we waited so long to kiss? Because I was scared silly to try to kiss her! I don't know what possessed me to turn my head to her that time. Must have been a muscle spasm. Whatever it was, I was glad I did it! I was also glad that our physical relationship with each other had a slow start. It was much easier to save ourselves for marriage since we didn't start making out the first day we met.

We read our Bibles together, we prayed together, and we gave all areas of our relationship to the Lord, especially our physical relationship.

One of the things I was especially thankful to my parents for was that they wouldn't let me go anywhere with Kristi alone our first year or so. She could come over to my house, and I could go to hers, as long as someone was there with us. Any dates had to be with other people, also. At first this bothered me. I felt like I was being treated like a little kid but in hindsight, I was glad for the restrictions. The longer we waited to start any kind of physical relationship, the easier it was to save ourselves for marriage. The first time I held hands it was like the Fourth of July, but soon after it lost its luster. The same was true for the first kiss. It was totally wonderful but soon after we had to kiss more and longer to get the same effect. We had to make a conscious effort to refrain from going any further in our physical relationship.

After she graduated, Kristi decided to work for the summer, and, when the fall came she didn't go to college. For the next three years she dealt with dating someone who was still in high school while she was out in the "real world." I grew to love my future wife more and more each week. I had a terrible self-image up to the point when I started dating her. Little by little she made me begin to like myself. If there is any one thing that she helped me with the most, it was my confidence. Today I am a very self-confident person. Those who know me well, say I am too self-confident. I can feel comfortable in any situation now, thanks to her. I am what I am, and, if you don't like me, then that's your problem. (See what I mean?)

Christmas of my senior year was coming up, and Kristi was dropping hints to me about a ring. She mentioned something to me about the people she worked with at General Motors kept asking where her ring was. I knew it was time to get her a ring and ask her to marry me! I picked out a ring, purchased it, and went home to make my plans. I knew I would give it to her at Christmas, but I also knew I needed to ask her dad's permission. I found myself over at her house one Sunday afternoon, and I was watching football with him. I had approached her mom earlier in the day and asked her if it would be okay if I married her daughter. I thought it best that I ask her mom first and then build up to her dad. Her mom looked at me and said she would be more than happy for us, but then added, "You know, Michael, she doesn't need our permission to get married." I figured that, but I wanted to make sure I honored her parents.

Finally it was time to face the man of the household. I went back in the living room, sat down on the couch across from his chair and began the longest afternoon of my life. I wasn't about to bother him while the game was on, so I had to wait for a commercial. Every time a commercial would come on, though, my heart would start beating wildly in my chest, my breath would get short, and, by the time I had worked up enough nerve to ask him, the game would come back on. This went on for perhaps an hour and a half. Finally, I worked up enough nerve to ask him. Before I knew it, I had gotten off the couch and found myself walking towards him. I was just ready to ask him when the game came back on.

AAAAARRGGGGHHHHHH!

Now what was I going to do? I was already at his chair, and had to think of something fast, so I knelt down next to him, and fumbled with my shoelaces like I had to tie them. I was stuck and didn't know what to do next. He looked at me out of the corner of his eye. My heart felt like it was going to leap out of my chest and flop around the room. He waited about a minute before he said, "Mike, is there something I can do for you?"

There I was on my knees in front of her dad, looking up at him like some lost puppy.

"I ah...I would...ah...

"Iwouldliketomarryyourdaughterifthatisokwithyou. Iboughtaringalreadyandwanttogiveittoher'causesomeguysatworkhadbeen askingheraboutaring. Iloveyourdaughterandwouldtakecareofher..."

My mouth was running a hundred miles an hour and I couldn't stop talking.

He looked down on me and told me he would like that. Then he patted me on the head, and I felt like the weight of the world had been lifted off of my shoulders. After I fetched his newspaper and slippers, I was able to enjoy the rest of the afternoon.

I wanted to give the ring to her at a special place, and I could think of no place more special to us than the land that my dad owned by Turtle Creek near Carver's Rock. Kristi and I loved it there, and I planned on us taking a moonlight stroll near the river with my future wife and our two dogs. My older brother got wind of my master plan about an hour before I put it into action.

"YOU ARE GOING TO GIVE HER THE RING WHERE?!" He was obviously upset about it. "YOU DON'T GIVE A WOMAN HER ENGAGEMENT RING BY A CREEK!"

I thought it would be perfect, but, what did I know? I had never done this before.

He told me that I should take her to a nice restaurant and give her the ring over dinner. That sounded fine and dandy to me, except that all my savings went to purchase the ring. Before I knew what was happening, he placed $50 in my hands, made reservations for me at a restaurant, and shoved me out the door.

So there we were. We ordered our meals and talked about whatever while we waited for our food to come. When it arrived and the waitress left, all we had to do was pray before we started to eat. It was our practice to hold hands while we prayed, so I reached my hands under the table and slipped the ring box into her outstretched fingers. Her eyes lit up...

I will always remember the look on her face when she opened the box and saw what it was...

"Kristi Conway, will you marry me?"

She said "yes", and the rest is history!

My plans were for us to get married right after my graduation party in June, but Kristi, in her infinite wisdom, suggested we wait until after my first year of college before getting married, which we did.

My wedding day was wonderful, but it went by so fast! We originally planned to sing to each other in our wedding, but as the time got closer Kristi got more and more nervous about it until she finally told me she couldn't do it; still, I decided to sing to her and picked out a song. The song I chose was entitled, "I Would Never Promise You."

I still remember the words by heart.

"I Could Never Promise You"
By Don Francisco

> I could never promise you with just my strength alone,
> but all my life I'd care for you and love you as my own.
> I've never seen the future. I only see today.
> Words that last a lifetime would be more than I could say.
> This love inside my heart today is more than mine alone.
> It never changes, never fails, and never seeks its own.
> And by the God who gives it and who lives in me and you.
> I know the words I speak today are words I'm going to do.
> So I stand before you now for all to hear and see.
> And promise you in Jesus' name a love He's given me.
> Through the years on earth and as eternity goes by

The life and love He's given us are never going to die.
The life and love He's given us are never going to die...

I was very nervous about the whole day, but I knew that if I could sing to my wife at my wedding, I could do anything. After I sang, the rest of the day seemed to go by in a blur.

The greatest gift that we gave to each other our wedding night was the gift of ourselves. Since we had waited to have sex until we got married, we were able to look into each other's eyes that night in the hotel room and say to each other, "I saved myself totally for you."

It is something we will never regret.

The rest of our lives up to this point are stories for another day, but I want my lovely bride to know this:

You are the most beautiful, caring, and compassionate person I have ever met. You have put up with so much in our thirteen years of marriage, and I am eternally grateful to God and to you for sticking with me. I have been a very selfish person through most of our lives together, and I hope that I have moved out of that stage and can now start to put you first. Thank you for two wonderful children, and for all that you sacrifice and do for us. You are the most wonderful wife and mother in all of God's creation, and I feel more in love with you today than I did when we first kissed.

I pray that we will wake up every day and "choose" to love each other, even when we don't feel like it. Continue to remember the verse we put on our wedding invitations: "...A cord of three strands is not easily broken" (Ecclesiastes 4:12). With Jesus in our life, we're going to make it.

I love you and want you to know that you are my best friend, and that you have made me the happiest man on earth.

Michael

# My Heart Aches

My heart aches tonight...

I ache for a wife and mother whose heart was broken and whose dreams were shattered when she heard the words, "I'm having an affair." A mother who doesn't have time to worry about herself, and is looking to her children's needs. As she goes about her daily life, she is stopped cold by images that make her physically sick. She tries not to let them flash through her head, but they still come. The images of her husband with another woman...While she was in the hospital, the day after the birth of their fourth child, and he was with another woman!!! The images stop her in her tracks, and she doubles over, while bile rises to her throat...

At times, every fiber of her being is crying out. Crying out for answers. Crying out for help. Crying out for the strength to face each day. A woman who has been forced into such activity that she doesn't have the proper time to think things through, let alone deal with the curve ball life has thrown her way. A woman who, while at work, is suddenly overwhelmed with emotion and has to find a private spot to let her grief run its course, or is forced to bury her feelings inside, just to meet her daily responsibilities.

My heart breaks for the woman who works full-time, and has been forced to take on a second job to help ends meet. The time she can spend with her little ones is filled with thoughts of what might have been. She's so tired. Oh so tired. "Mom, could you read us the story?" She tries concentrating on a children's book...and wakes up with a jerk of her head. "Mom! You said you would read us the story!"

I ache for these women who feel a sense of betrayal so deep, that their self-worth has been stripped away to expose the nerve endings of their inner beings. When the air of reality washes over these nerves, they scream inside from the pain, and then slowly return to the dull ache that never goes away...

I ache for a teenage girl, whose sense of security has been stolen, who is torn between her mom and dad. One moment she is angry, but before she can deal with her emotion, it changes to confusion, then sadness, then bitterness. "WHY DOES THIS HAVE TO HAPPEN TO ME?! WHY GOD?! WHY DID YOU LET THIS HAPPEN TO MY FAMILY!?"

Which parent to believe? Which one to trust? Who do I blame?

"Maybe it is because of me..." She tries to push the thoughts away.

She deals with it in the only way she knows how. She locks her feelings inside in a place that will never see the light of day...But she is sadly mistaken if she thinks she can avoid dealing with her feelings. Someday, somewhere, they will come out, and if they haven't been dealt with...I shudder at the consequences.

She deals with the stares at school. She hears the whispers. She hears the rumors.

She doesn't want to talk about it. "Why do people keep asking me if I want to talk about it!! Just leave me alone!!"

But when she goes to bed, and tries to find some much-needed rest, her thoughts haunt her. She can be strong in front of her friends and family, but when she is all alone at night, she lets her guard down...She thought it was for the best. Her mom and dad were constantly fighting! If they get a divorce, there will finally be peace in the house...but there is no peace, only an open wound, as another family is torn apart. A wound that is ever so slow in healing, and leaves scars that will affect everyone for the rest of their lives. The silence of the night is broken by her sobs.

My heart aches for the little children. Beautiful children, who have been thrown this way and that way, as their parents try to get back at each other.

"You have a new mommy now."

"Don't tell your father I let you do that."

"Why can't you be a big boy for mommy and stop crying?"

"If that is the way you are going to act, you can go live with your idiot of a father!"

I cry for these children who are growing up way before their time, who are being forced into things they should never have to deal with at a young age. Children who just can't be children anymore.

I cry for the little boy at his soccer match. He scans the crowd before his game looking for his daddy. He's doesn't see his face. The match starts. Every chance he gets, he looks toward the parking lot to see if his dad is coming.

"He told me he wouldn't miss this for the world!"

The little candles of light in the boy's eyes start to flicker, and then die out.

Another promise broken. Another scar made. Another life affected.

"What do you mean he cried when I didn't come? I know I told him I would be there, but he has to understand that I have a life, too. I don't have to be there every time, do I?"

But as the father hangs up the phone, he knows he let his son down. If he goes to the game, his new wife will get on him. She doesn't want him to be there. She knows his first wife will want to sit by him as they share their son's game. He hates dealing with the yelling, so he takes the easy way out.

My heart aches for a father and husband. A husband who is at home while his bride is gone late into the night. Sometimes she doesn't even come home. He plays with his young daughter, but his thoughts are elsewhere. As he tucks her in at night, he forces a smile, kisses her, and tries to make up still another story as to why Mommy didn't come home. Does she even care about him anymore? Does she even care what it is doing to her daughter?

I ache for this woman, also. She runs from her problems, goes from this person to that, as she searches for something to fill the void in her life. She will look back on this time and weep bitterly. Weep for the times she missed out with her young daughter. Weep when she realizes that she had everything she was searching for right at home.

I weep for a husband who felt he had no choice but to leave his wife and children because of too many fights, too many conflicts, too much pain. He wonders if he made the right decision, but he tells himself it was for the best. He tells himself that if he stays, things will become worse, so he tells his wife and children he is leaving.

"I just don't love her anymore. We can't make it work."

He wonders what this will do to his children, how this decision will affect his life. He wonders if there was any way he could have made it work.

I hurt for a husband who listened to the world, a husband who once stood before his bride and promised to be faithful...promised for better or for worse. The words had no meaning, and now he thinks he is rid of his problems. He listens to the lies that come from his mouth: "I'll make a new life with this woman. I'll be happy. I owe it to myself to be happy. The kids are young; they will adjust."

Although he is now with a different woman, he finds the problems he ran from are still with him. He tries to tell himself otherwise, but he knows now. So many lives damaged, so many promises have been broken that some mornings he can't even face himself in the mirror.

My heart is torn for a wife and mother who is left to cope, whose life crumbled around her when she heard the words, "I'm leaving you." She feels the pain with every heart beat, and is left crawling on the floor of existence, slowly searching for the pieces of the life she thought she had. She ponders what is wrong with her and is left to deal with the feeling that she is not attractive enough anymore. She thinks, "If only I had done this, he would have stayed." She saw it coming, but never thought it would happen. The fights were more frequent, the intimacy was gone, the communication was nonexistent but she never thought it would happen. She is left reeling and dizzy, as she searches for answers, and tries to untangle the mess her life has become. Some days she calls out to God and wonders how she will make it through another day.

I ache for a woman who purposely set out to destroy a family. Oh, she doesn't call it that. No, she tells herself that he obviously wasn't happy with his wife; she is the only one who can make him happy. The delusion continues as she plans her new life and family with this man she slept with while he was still married, meeting in secret places, lying to cover what was going on. Never once does it occur to her that he will betray his vows once again.

"No way will he cheat on me. He loves me!" she tells herself.

That's what his first wife thought...

I weep for these families...I pray for these families...

I ache...

Too many lives are being destroyed. Too many futures are being snuffed out. Too many children have no place to feel secure, no place to run to when the cares of the world grow too burdensome. Home is not safe anymore. Home is not...home anymore.

Kristi and I have seen so many families broken apart that we often wonder if it might happen to us someday. What chance does any marriage have in today's world?

However, we refuse to get discouraged.

I know that God can change lives, and heal emotional wounds. I know that God can impress upon a young couple to honor their vows. I know that He can take a hopeless situation and bring people back together again. I have seen it. I have seen couples give their marriages to God, and seemingly hopeless situations become strong marriages again. But it takes work. Lots of work! In fact, if we knew before we got married how much work it was going to be, I don't know if we would have walked the aisle together. I honestly believe, though, when people love each other the way God intends, it becomes easier. When I treat Kristi with love, honor, and respect, she wants to do the same for me. When I stop trying to change what I think is wrong with her and instead change the things I know are wrong with me, our relationship improves. The more she looks to my needs, the more I want to look to her needs. When we stop listening to the world, and start listening to what God says about relationships, miraculous things happen!

The most important thing my wife and I have learned in our thirteen years of marriage is that love is not a feeling; it is a decision.

Let me write that again:

Love is not a feeling. It is a decision.

Kristi chose to love me early in our marriage. If our marriage were based on how she felt, she would have left me years ago. While I have never cheated on her, I was not there for her emotionally, and I looked totally to my own needs and wants. But through it all, Kristi chose to love me. She chose to love me when I hurt her with my words, when I sacrificed her for my side of the family, when I placed my athletic endeavors above our relationship. When the romantic feelings were gone and dead, she chose to love me. When I chose to love her back, the feelings she thought were dead came alive again! You see, when people choose to love, the feelings follow.

God worked through Kristi to get my attention and to start making me into the man of God I needed to be. I am still a piece of clay that God is molding and shaping, and I still have a long way to go, but I know that our relationship grows stronger every day. We still have our setbacks, but God will continue to make us into the husband and wife he wants us to be.

My heart continues to ache for the situations we have seen in the lives of those around us, situations that have no winners. However, I have learned something from each broken family that I see. I have learned that it can happen to anyone, including Kristi and me. With each ache that I feel, I develop a stronger resolve to make my marriage work. I learn to depend on God more in my relationship. I vow that I will make a loving home for my children to grow up in, no matter what personal wants I have to set aside. Most of all, I am forever grateful for the incredible wife that God picked out for me in advance, and for the Godly men and women that He has placed in our lives as mentors, friends, and examples.

This world needs spouses who will honor their vows, parents who will place the needs of their children before theirs, and children who have a loving home in which to grow and blossom into the spouses and parents of the future. It is time to break the patterns. It is time for people to stand at an altar, look into their soulmate's eyes, and tell each other that divorce is not an option, to vow that they will make it work, no matter how hard it may be at times, to stand up to what the world so enticingly whispers in their ears. The grass is not greener on the other side. If everyone takes care of their own lawn and garden, as they watch it grow and bloom they won't even be able to see the other side!

# Promises Kept

By Kristi Powers

**In a world where so many lives are being torn apart by divorces and heartaches, comes a story of a father and a daughter, and a promise that was kept.**

My father was not a sentimental man. I don't remember him ever "ooohhing" or "ahhing" over something I made as a child. Don't get me wrong; I knew that my dad loved me, but getting all mushy-eyed was not his thing. I learned that he showed me love in other ways.

There was one particular time in my life when this became real to me...

I always believed that my parents had a good marriage, but just before I, the youngest of four children, turned sixteen, my belief was sorely tested. My father, who used to share in the chores around the house, gradually started becoming despondent. From the time he came home from his job at the factory to the time he went to bed, he hardly spoke a word to my mom or us kids. The strain on my mom and dad's relationship was very evident. However, I was not prepared for the day that Mom sat my siblings and me down and told us that Dad had decided to leave. All that I could think of was that I was going to become a product of a divorced family. It was something I never thought possible, and it grieved me greatly. I kept telling myself that it wasn't going to happen, and I went totally numb when I knew my dad was really leaving. The night before he left, I stayed up in my room for a long time. I prayed and I cried—and I wrote a long letter to my Dad. I told him how much I loved him and how much I would miss him. I told him that I was praying for him and wanted him to know that, no matter what, Jesus and I loved him. I told him that I would always and forever be his Krissie...his

Noodles. As I folded my note, I stuck in a picture of me with a saying I had always heard. "Anyone can be a father, but it takes someone special to be a daddy."

Early the next morning, as my Dad left our house, I sneaked out to the car and slipped my letter into one of his bags.

Two weeks went by with hardly a word from my father. Then, one afternoon, I came home from school to find my mom sitting at the dining room table waiting to talk to me. I could see in her eyes that she had been crying. She told me that Dad had been there and that they had talked for a long time. They decided that there were things that the both of them could and would change—and that their marriage was worth saving. Mom then turned her focus to my eyes—"Kristi, Dad told me that you wrote him a letter. Can I ask what you wrote to him?" I found it hard to share with my mom what I had written from my heart to my dad. I mumbled a few words and shrugged. Mom said, "Well, Dad said that when he read your letter, it made him cry. It meant a lot to him and I have hardly ever seen your dad cry. After he read your letter, he called to ask if he could come over to talk. Whatever you said really made a difference to your dad."

A few days later my dad was back, this time to stay. We never talked about the letter, my dad and I. I guess I always figured that it was something that was a secret between us.

My parents went on to be married a total of thirty-six years before my dad's early death at the age of fifty-three cut short their lives together. In the last sixteen years of my parent's marriage I, and all those who knew my mom and dad, witnessed one of the truly "great" marriages. Their love grew stronger every day, and my heart swelled with pride as I saw them grow closer together...

When Mom and Dad received the news from the doctor that his heart was deteriorating rapidly, they took it hand in hand, side by side, all the way.

After Dad's death, we had the most unpleasant task of going through his things. I have never liked this task and opted to run errands so I did not have to be there while most of the things were divided and boxed up. When I got back from my errand, my brother said "Kristi, Mom said to give this to you. She said you would know what it meant." As I looked down into his outstretched hand, it was then that I knew the impact of my letter that day so long ago. In my brother's hand was my picture that I had given my dad that day. My unsentimental dad, who never let his emotions get the best of him, my dad, who almost never outwardly showed his love for me, had kept the one thing that meant so much to him and me. I sat down and the tears began to flow, tears that I thought had dried up from the grief of his death, but that had now found new life as I realized what I had meant to him. Mom told me that Dad kept both the picture and that letter his whole life. I have a box in my home that I call the "Dad box". In it are so many things that remind me of my dad. I pull that picture out every once in a while and remember. I remember a promise that was made many years ago between a young man and his bride on their wedding day, and I remember the unspoken promise that was made between a father and his daughter...

A promise kept.

*****

**Connor Short Take**

Grandma was talked into having a pretend sword fight with our 2-year-old, Connor, so they picked up their plastic swords and faced off. Grandma assumed the proper fencing position and yelled out, "On Guard" in her best French accent. Connor, without skipping a beat, also assumed his best fencing position and yelled out, "I'm Jesus!" He figured if Grandma was going to be God (he thought she said, "I'm God!") when she dueled with him, he had better be Jesus to keep the match fair...

# Taking Off the Mask

Many will recall a story I wrote a while ago called "Tuxedo Swimming", a humorous story about my experience taking my son swimming at the local YMCA. It was sent out by Lee Simonson, the founder of Heartwarmers.com, and I was overwhelmed with e-mails from those who had read it. I was quite humbled by what everyone wrote as I went through hundreds of e-mails that first day alone, and all of them were very encouraging. Then, just before I went to work that night I read one from a lady who was not very happy with me.

She said: "I just read your piece in Heartwarmers. My first and only thought was: Why did you ask your wife to call the YMCA? You have enough time to write this story, but you can't be bothered to make a simple phone call yourself? Men like you who treat their 'lovely wives' like secretaries make me angry. It's clear you are really full of yourself."

I went from flying with the eagles on top of the mountain, to plummeting at breakneck speed to the bottom of the mud and slime-filled swamp. Literally hundreds of positive e-mails were wiped out by one negative one.

As I was taking my forty-minute drive to work that night, I had a lot of time to think about it. My head kept telling me that this person didn't know me, and that, if she did, she wouldn't feel this way but my heart felt like it had been cut by a knife. Her words hurt me, and the harder I tried to think only of the positive ones, my mind was pulled like a piece of metal to a huge magnet back to what she had written.

What is it about our nature that makes us dwell so much more on negative things than on positive ones? I had enough positive feedback to last me for a year, but I continually beat myself with thoughts of her note. It brought my attention to the old saying, "It takes twenty positive comments to make up for just one negative comment."

It took me a day or so before I was able to get it out of my mind. My first thought was to e-mail her back and tell her that I had my wife type it up as I did not have the time to respond to her but I decided not to.

After a few days I did write her back, explaining that I work third shift, that the YMCA is open only after I go to sleep for the day, that I love and respect my wife and am very appreciative of all she does for me in raising our kids, helping me with many aspects of my video business, and the myriad of other things she does on a daily basis.

However, I also thanked her for her openness and honesty, and for taking the time to respond to me. I believe one should always look for a grain of truth in every criticism, and it brought my attention to all the overlooked things that my wife does for me.

It also made me more aware of my words and how they can hurt people. As a husband, father, coach, and human being, I know how powerful my words are to my wife, kids, players, and those I come into contact with every day. For example, my coaching philosophy is based on getting players to play hard because they want to and because they respect and love me, not because I am yelling and screaming at them for what they do wrong. If I have to correct a player, I try to sandwich anything of a corrective nature with two positive things they do well.

For example: "Jamie Rusch, you are an awesome point guard and I am so thankful for the opportunity to coach a young lady like you. The one thing you need to work on to make you a better player is using your left hand to dribble and pass. When you get better at that, you are going to be simply unstoppable!" As compared to: "Jamie! When are you going to learn to use your left hand!! We are not in junior high anymore!! I can't believe that you haven't learned that by now!! If you don't start getting better at it, I'm going to sit your butt down for the rest of the stinkin' season!"

I can make or break one of my players just by what I say to them. It was a responsibility that scared me to death when I first started coaching, but it is something I look forward to every day now in a gym.

Words are powerful.

As I dwelt more and more on what the lady wrote to me, I thought about the stinging, hurtful words I say in my own house that would shock my basketball players who only know me as a positive coach. You see, the ones I love the most are the ones I hurt the most. I put on my positive face when I leave my house, but when I get home, sometimes I take off my mask, hang it by the door, and become someone I am not very proud of. I am getting better at learning to treat my wife and kids with the same love, respect, and honor that I treat those outside of my home, but I still fail my family at times. If for nothing else, I thank that woman for sending me that e-mail and making me more aware of this.

Words...Little ink spots on a piece of paper, or syllables uttered by a tongue. They don't seem like much sometimes, but they are a powerful force that can be used to build people up or tear people down.

I, for one, am going to try harder to build up. I know I will fail at times, but Lord willing, I will get better.

*****

**Caleb Short Take**

The other day we bought Caleb some new toys, not just any new toys, mind you, but, as Caleb says, "My new Lion King II: Simba's Pride toys!" Unfortunately our wonderful three-year-old was beginning to experiment with the habit of spitting, so I told him that if he spit again, I was going to take away his new Lion King II: Simba's Pride toys. He looked up at me and thought for a second, then responded by saying, "When you take my Lion King II: Simba's Pride toys away, I can get something better!"

Somehow the whole lesson was lost on him.

# My Forever Friend

By Kristi Powers

"I've dreamed of meeting her all my life...a bosom friend—an intimate friend, you know—a really kindred spirit to whom I can confide my inmost soul."—Anne of Green Gables

It is a friendship that almost didn't happen...but God in his infinite wisdom knew what I needed in my life—one true friend who knew everything about me, thorns and all, but still invited me to share and grow with her in this thing called life.

Len and Kathy went to the orphanage that crisp fall day with a slip of paper in their hand to see the baby boys, in the hopes of adding one to their family of three. But instead of a bouncing baby boy, the staff brought down one chubby molasses-eyed girl. Realizing their mistake, they started to take the baby girl back to the nursery. Just before they started climbing the stairs, the dark-haired beauty chose to smile at Len with the biggest, toothless grin in all the world. Right then and there she captured their hearts. Their immediate response was "NO, WE'LL TAKE HER!" They knew that baby Rachel, as she was soon to be called, was meant for them and only them. That angelic baby was to become my kindred-spirit, my forever friend.

I vividly remember the moment I first met her at the age of four. Rachel's oldest sister and my sister were getting together to play, and, as my mom dropped off my sister at their house, there she was, the dark-haired beauty in contrast to my fair blonde locks. She was sitting on her swing and my first thought was that she was the most beautiful girl I had ever seen in my four years of life. From that moment on we were to be friends...bosom buddies.

One day in junior high we were riding home together from basketball practice and Rachel's mom and she were talking about Rachel's future in basketball. Rachel had developed a non-cancerous tumor on her thigh which had been giving her quite a lot of pain. As we drove along that winter day, Rachel reached for my hand in the dark. I sat with her as she and her mom talked about the possibility of her giving up basketball. That is the way our friendship has always been, and I always hope it will be. When the dark times come, we cling to each other and hang on until the light comes again.

Rachel and I are mostly opposites. Rachel was the one who would be prepared and study hard for the PSAT tests for school. I would be beside her getting bored, circling answers just because I felt like it. Rachel was Clinton High School's class valedictorian, and the first girl in our state renowned basketball program to be on the varsity team as a freshman. She was as intense as a person could possibly be. I, on the other hand, went to school to socialize and have fun and was easy-going in my demeanor and personality. I would often show up late for school throughout our senior year as I had a first hour study hall. I would meet Rachel and the principal in the hallway as I entered the school doors. I would say hi to them both and smile my most engaging smile at Gene Harsevoort, the principal. He would just shake his head and smile at his troublesome student. Those antics earned me the class award for "Most Tardy", while Rachel received the "Most Likely to Succeed" award.

After graduation from high school, Rachel already had her life planned out before her; I felt confusion over my future and was scared. The day that high school started the next fall, I heard the bus as it made its usual pass by my house. From there it would rumble down the road past Rachel's house, then turn around and head back past my house again and on to school. I don't ever remember feeling so unsure of myself as I did that day. As I sprawled in my bed, the abrupt ring of the phone dragged me from my thoughts. I picked up the receiver and it was Rachel saying, "It sure feels weird to not be on that bus, doesn't it?" It was only one of many uncanny moments we have shared throughout our thirty years of friendship.

I can't remember a crucial or happy moment in my life that Rachel has not been beside me, cheering me on, holding my hand, and pointing me towards Christ, sometimes even giving me a swift kick in the butt. Our friendship is one that even my husband does not understand. Although we are three hours away from each other, we just know when the other needs something. Somehow God has orchestrated our friendship in a way that we will instinctively know when a phone call or card is needed to let the other know that we are there. One time we even sent the exact same card to each other ON THE SAME DAY.

When my father died four years ago, Rachel took time off work and stayed throughout the visitation and funeral the next day. Her eyes were constantly on me and any time I was sitting alone for an extended period of time, I would find her sitting or standing next to me, holding my hand or just listening to me. My biggest tears fell when she reached me in the receiving line. "Rachel would know how I feel," I said to myself, "for she is a sister of my heart and my dad loved her like he loved his own kids." I knew she would feel and share in my pain, and she did.

The only regret I have is that in the last few years Rachel has been there for me much more than I have been there for her. I can't count how many times I have called her crying or hurting and she has NEVER, EVER given me the feeling that I was bothering her, or that she felt that it was time I got over the things hurting me so deeply. I can only pray that I will be there for her—be that sounding board, confidante, and friend that she has been for me.

It has been thirty years now. All these thoughts are in my head and heart as I try in my feeble way to thank Rachel for all that she has been and always will be in my life. My forever friend, if you had not been born and your birth mom had not given you up out of her love; if your mom and dad had not seen you that day and had you not captured their hearts, my life would not have been complete until I had found you. You, Rachel, are my one true friend, my forever friend. I thank you from the bottom of my heart.

# Hung on Every Word

I was hired to produce and show a video for the Wisconsin Basketball Coaches Association's Hall of Fame banquet this past Saturday, and everything seemed to be going wrong. I was stressed and a bit nervous about how things were turning out.

In the midst of the chaos, I started looking for those coaches and people I knew. After making some small talk, I saw someone very special to me from across the huge hall. I had not seen Gena Gilbertson in a long time. She was a former player from the basketball program I coach in and she was attending with her mom, Donna, and her dad, Whitey.

Whitey is the head coach at Clinton High School, and was there picking up an award for his 500th victory. (I'm "just" 340 wins behind him and it should only take me thirty years to catch up to him!)

Gena is the type of person who just lights up a room. She is a beautiful young lady, but it is her personality and her beaming face, which captures and holds everyone's attention. Kristi and I remember when she was a little girl. When Kristi was in high school and played basketball for Whitey, Gena would bring her Barbie dolls to her dad in the middle of an intense game and ask him to help her dress them! Believe me, anyone who knows Whitey would be laughing until their stomach hurt right now! Gena will always be special to both of us, and I was so glad to see her again.

I made my way through the crowd and plopped myself down on the only chair left at their table. I started asking her how college was going, but she kept steering the conversation back to what was going on with me. She asked what was new in my life, and I started telling her about my writing and how I was going to have some stories published that coming spring. Her whole face lit up and I could genuinely sense that she was happy for me. Then she asked how my Kristi was doing, then how Caleb and Connor were doing, and then if I was looking forward to coaching this coming basketball season. She asked question after question and, before long, I was under her spell. My worries about showing the video melted away. She made me feel like I was the most important person in the room as she hung on every word I said.

I realized she was doing something I had learned from a Sunday School teacher a long time ago: the art of listening and being a good friend. If people want to develop relationships, they need to stop talking about themselves and let the other person do the talking. To make friends, just ask people questions and get them talking about themselves. There is nothing we like better as humans than to talk about ourselves.

Normally I would be ashamed that I had done most of the talking and had not asked enough questions to get her to communicate to me how her life was going, but I wasn't. I just realized a better listener had bested me. It wasn't long before I broke her spell, and steered the conversation back to what was going on in her life.

This is the one time I didn't feel badly about doing most of the talking. When it came to listening, I had met the master and there was no shame in coming in second this day.

We love you, Gena!

# Letting Go

There is a beautiful story I heard once about a child playing with a vase his mother had left on the table for a few moments. When the mother turned at the sound of her son crying she saw that his hand was in the vase, apparently stuck. She tried to help him and pulled and pulled until the child cried out in pain, but the hand was stuck fast. How would they get it out?

The father suggested breaking the vase, but it was quite valuable, and the child's hand might be cut in the process. Yet he knew that, if all else failed, there would be no other alternative, so he said to the boy, "Now, let's make one more try. Open your hand and stretch your fingers out straight, like I'm doing, and then pull!"

"But Dad," said the boy, "If I do that, I'll lose my penny!"

The boy had had a coin in his hand all the time, holding it securely in his tight little fist, and wasn't prepared to open his hand and lose the penny. Once he opened his hand, it came out of the vase easily.

I know that in the same way I hold on to things in my life that I think are so important to me, even though that holding on causes problems. Early in my marriage all I cared about was becoming the best volleyball player in the state of Wisconsin. One year, while Kristi was working second shift at General Motors, I played in 1400 games, competing four nights a week and forty out of fifty-two weekends. My team won over 1000 games, thirty-two of the forty tournaments, and two gold medals at the Badger State Games. Great success on the volleyball court, but a huge loss in my relationship with my Kristi. I remember being so frustrated when she would ask me not to play on a certain weekend.

When we would do things together, I would constantly be thinking about how I could be competing instead, and, as I held so tightly to becoming a good player, I was losing my wife.

Gradually God started getting my attention, and when we had Caleb, I began to realize how self-centered I was being, and how I was working so hard at something that in the whole scheme of life, meant two things: Didley & Squat!

When I finally let go, I looked back at what I had done and was ashamed. Not only did I show my wife she wasn't the most important thing to me, but I missed out on a lot of relationship-building time. My life is so much richer now that I am not a slave to that drive to be the best player possible. I still love to compete, and, with all the great players I have surrounded myself with, we can still go anywhere in the tri-state area and expect to be in the finals, but now it's not the all-consuming fire.

What is it in life that you are afraid to let go of? What has a hold on you and is keeping you from enjoying the richness of life that God intended? Let go and watch how God moves in and frees you to be all He intended you to be!

My Kristi put up with all these things and continued to love me, still had faith that I would become the man I should be, and stuck with me. She's a special lady indeed! I still have a way to go and some growing up to do, but I owe her more than I can ever repay!

*****

**Caleb Short Take**

Kristi told me that she went by Caleb's room one day and he was singing about me. I started getting warm fuzzies in my tummy thinking of how sweet it was that he was singing about his daddy. She told me his words were, "I love my daddy, I love my daddy, I love my daddy..." By this time I was swelling with pride. His next verse, however, was, "BUT I DON'T KNOW WHY! NO, I DON'T KNOW WHY!"

Then back to, "I love my daddy, I love my daddy..."

# Meet Me By The Sea

(In dedication to my Aunts, Uncles, and their spouses.)

**By Kristi Powers**

I stand on a sandy beach, the very place my grandpa and his best friend stood fifty years ago as they stopped over during a plane trip to Florida. I never knew my grandpa, but I have seen the photograph many times that captured them smiling and having the time of their lives as they enjoyed the pristine land and air of Palm Pavilion.

Both have since passed away, and the land has changed much in half a century. My aunts, uncles, and my grandpa's best friend's son have come to gather in the same place. They lift their drinks high as the deep orange glow of the sun, setting over the Gulf of Mexico, splashes upon their faces. They toast to what was, and to what will never be again. After they sip from their glasses, they turn to my siblings and me and ask, "In fifty years, will you kids come back here and have a toast for us?"

I smile and say, "Of course, but only if you come also."

I am aware of the futility of such a response, yet my mind cannot grasp life without these colorful characters of my youth, the ones who have had a part in shaping and forming so much of who I am...

Aunt Janet—
I have the fondest memories of playing in her basement. My cousins, siblings, and I would spend hours perfecting our "dance routine." We would then call all our relatives down to perform before them. It was her stability, her balanced life, and her creativity that helped me to understand what quality time really costs—only my willingness.

Uncle Denny—
Denny followed his father's love for flying. I cannot see a single-engine plane in the sky without remembering all the times he surprised

81

my siblings and me by flying low over our house. Most times it was our only notice that he was back in the states and coming for a visit!

Aunt Jo, or "Silly" Aunt Jo, as my Caleb calls her—
Jo, whose love for kids, games, and kindness, which comes from devotion to her Creator, has truly enriched our lives.

My beloved Uncle Gary—
Gary may not even be aware of all the roles he played and the way he influenced the lives of thirteen nieces and nephews. He was grandpa, friend and mentor. Where would I be today if I had not had my Uncle Gary to read me books, take me on long walks, or let me put his long locks in ponytails?

And lastly, my own dear mother—
Mom's lasting legacy will be her gifts of laughter, unconditional love, and faith in Christ.

I ponder all of this as I leave them and take a walk by the sea. The sound of their laughter drifts away as the lull of the waves calls to me. The dolphins dance as I think of the changes the land has gone through in fifty years. The waves have done their duty, creating more sand and beach on which to walk. Each grain's beauty is full of memories of time long past. I, like the land, have been forever changed. I take the good from those who have come before me, and I have learned...

Fifty more years have now passed...

Come with me cousins, brother and sisters. Let us raise our toast high in the air and remember those who made us the way we are.

Come, meet me by the sea.

# Anniversary Song

June 11, 1999

Dear Kristi,

As I look back on our eleven years of marriage, I am overwhelmed with thoughts and feelings. Deep feelings. Feelings that wash over me in warm waves. Feelings that leave tiny hills on my skin.

I feel gratitude for you sticking with me and for being so eternally patient as you waited for me to grow up...for all the nights you cried yourself to sleep, hoping and praying that someday I might put your needs first instead of my selfish wants...for all the times you felt unprotected by me emotionally as we dealt with things early in our marriage...for carrying the financial burden for seven years as I tried to figure out what to do with my life...for all the times I have given of myself to other people and then come home and offered you the "leftovers"...for going before our Heavenly Father in prayer, and lifting me up, even when my hurtful words have made deep cuts that took many months to heal. For all that you do and all you have done to keep our marriage working. I am amazed at your unselfishness. Amazed that you have stuck it out with me, and for that I am thankful.

Thankful...

Thankful for the incredible example you are of Godly love that is based on a decision and not your feelings...love that has looked for the best in me all these years...love that is unconditional...love that has seen past the immaturity...love that has molded and shaped me into a better person. Love that has sifted through the stress of my working a third shift job and running a video production business. Oh, to have half of your boundless capacity for real love. I stand in awe at your ability to love people...

Awe...

I don't know of a better word to describe how I feel about you. I stand in awe as I watch you raise our two boys. My mouth drops open as I watch you go through your life as a mother: the energy that is exerted, the compassion and firmness in discipline, the daily and nightly grind you go through pouring your heart and soul into these two little gifts from God. I get a bubbly feeling inside when I hear someone talk about our boys in a positive manner, and I know they are special because of what you have invested in them. You stumble into bed each night, knowing that you are going to be up at least a few times in the night with Connor, yet each morning you dig down into your reserves and pour your energy once again into nurturing and caring for our little ones. Our children are wonderful! I don't care who hears it or what they think about a father bragging about his children. Our children are wonderful because of the hours you have invested in their lives, and the example you set for them every day. My children will know how special their mother is. They will instinctively know it, but, just in case they don't, I will make a point of telling them often. They will look back on their childhood with warm feelings and memories...

Memories...

Little flashes of "life" come to me as I go about my daily routine. A song might trigger them, or perhaps a fragrant scent. Sometimes it's merely a word or phrase. I go from the mundane task I am doing and am transported to another time. A feeling of contentment and satisfaction comes over me as I relive these moments: spending time in the hospital as you brought our children into this world, the image of you holding Caleb and Connor for the first time. I hear the heavenly sound of your singing and run my fingers through your hair. I see Caleb talk with his many little hand gestures and watch him make everything in his life into an "Oscar winning production." I listen to Connor saying, "Ohhhhhhhh," feel the softness of the back of his hair and smell his baby lotion. I watch him pulling himself along the floor without using his back legs to crawl and picture his lips when he is sleeping. Over all I hear the music in your laugh, and see the love in your liquid eyes...

These things pass through my mind on any given day, and I stop and thank the Lord for the life He has given me. I owe so much to you, Kristi, and I love the life we have made with each other. While the memories create such tremendous contentment in my life, I also visualize the little flashes of life that haven't happened yet.

The future...

I look forward to walking away from the third shift job and being able to hold you in my arms as we lie in bed and fall asleep listening to the crickets. I can't wait to wake up in the morning instead of heading off to bed. I visualize moving from the middle of town and having our kids grow up surrounded by woods and fields and Caleb coming home with a frog in each pocket. I see us taking long walks, enjoying the sounds of the birds, the smell of wildflowers, and looking up at the millions of stars from the deck of our house in the country. I envision holding our daughter "Kelsey" for the first time and crying tears of joy. One day we will watch our last child head off to college, knowing full well that a portion of our lives will never be the same. I will love you more every day and we'll become closer as we intertwine our hopes, thoughts, and feelings. We'll grow old, but I won't care, as long as you are by my side every step of the way as we build our dreams into reality.

Reality...

My reality right now is a dream for me. I can deal with the long workweeks, the stress, and sometimes the exhaustion. They pale in comparison to what the Lord has blessed me with. I will still dream, but I am content. Everyday problems come, but they soon melt away with the coo of my infant, the hug of my three-year-old, and the tender kiss of my bride.

Bring on what troubles you have, World. My Kristi is by my side...

Happy Anniversary, my love!
Michael

# The Gift of Life

By Kristi Powers

"For you created my inmost being; you knit me together in my mother's womb. I praise you because I am fearfully and wonderfully made; your works are wonderful, I know that full well." — Psalms 139:13,14

It is that time of year again...the time for rainy spring days, the smell of budding flowers, and the sound of chatter on the softball field...

As I watch the tear-stained eighteen-year-old, I want to hug out all of the sadness and frustration she is feeling and tell her how much I love her. Tonight may be the last softball game of her high school career. A career cut short because a nagging knee injury needs surgery so that she can be ready to fulfill her athletic scholarship at college. As I gaze upon her face, I cannot help but think of how fortunate I have been to know this beautiful young lady. However, I know how easily her song could have been one that was unsung...

It was almost nineteen years ago that a teenager trembled as she tearfully said to her mother and father the words that every parent dreads..."Mom, Dad, I'm pregnant."

What a frightening time for a nineteen-year-old as she is just starting her adult life and already facing an uncertain future. What devastation for the parents as this is the last thing they would have chosen for their daughter. Thoughts of "we have failed her" to "I am too young to be a grandparent", fill their minds. In a heartbeat the atmosphere in the house becomes strained and the following nights are long for the teen as she drenches her pillow with tears. Tears that come only when she thinks no one can see or hear her.

Many try to persuade her to keep her options open, but there is only one choice for this determined teen. The little life within her has now become her responsibility, and she will sacrifice all she has to see that this precious being grows to be the young man or woman God intended him/her to be. She is at peace with herself, and the choice she has made...

A baby's first cries fill the air and an exhausted but proud, teenage mom holds her young daughter for the first time. She is inexperienced, but is determined to provide for her priceless daughter the best way that she can. If the first few days are any indication, she has a tough hill to climb. Because of no insurance, she leaves the hospital early and takes her daughter home, but the baby girl develops jaundice, and they are forced back to the hospital. Her pediatrician tells her to leave the baby in their care and to go home and rest. "You have got to be kidding me!" she exclaims, refusing to leave her baby girl for even a moment. Something inside her clicks, and, with a determination that surpasses anything she has felt up to this point, she comes to grips with the situation. "You are a mom now. Deal with it," she quietly tells herself.

Life is not easy and many hopes and plans for the future are set aside. The early years are filled with tests and trials but it is a time in her life that she wouldn't trade for anything. During those rough days and nights, she need only look at this tender creation God has given her to realize that the best things in life are right before her in the smile, the coo, and the laugh of this darling baby girl.

Those eighteen years have flown by, and I ponder all of these things as we slowly walk away from the softball diamond today. I think about all the joy this baby girl, who is now a young woman herself, has brought into my life and to those around her. I remember all the basketball and softball games that we as her family have sat through, proudly cheering her on. Not only is she the best all-around female athlete I have ever seen, she is also one of the classiest and I am most proud of who she is off the court. She conducts herself with grace and humility and shows kindness to all who cross her path. I cannot imagine life without my Jen, my darling eighteen-year-old niece.

Tonight my heart is bursting with pride, love, and joy for this remarkable being who came into our lives. I shudder to think if she had not been born. How different our family would have been, not to mention the lives of an untold number of people whom she has touched in her everyday life.

A scared but determined teenage mom made a tough decision all those years ago, and through it, gave us all the gift of Jen.

# Close To You

**By Kristi Powers**

Happy Birthday, Kayla!

How could it be that you turn ten today? It seems like only yesterday that I stood outside your hospital room and listened to your entrance into this world (Boy did you cry)! When I first saw you, Kayla, I loved you. Never had a baby captured my heart as you did mine. At our family gatherings I would hold you before me and watch your every move. I would stand amazed and proud at every yawn, smile or gurgle. Our family would tease me that all you would ever remember from your infancy was that big head of mine in front of your face. I would stand and scoff at their cynicism and say, "You just wait! When my niece is older, I will be the one laughing when she chooses me as her favorite." The day I remember most though, Kayla, is the day that we bonded for all time. It has been my secret to this day, and now I will share it with you:

When you were about six months old, I babysat you at Grandma and Grandpa Conway's house while your mom and dad went out to dinner with them. It was a crisp fall night. I could hear the crickets singing their nightly lullaby, and I bundled you up in a blanket and took you outside. Your bright blue eyes stared intently into mine, and they matched the fullness of the moon as it splashed upon your countenance. I took you around the yard and showed you all the places where your dad and I used to play together as children. I showed you Aunt Kimmy's favorite tree and the barn where your dad and I shared many adventures as we watched the new life that sprung among the animals there. I shared with you how your daddy was my best friend for those earlier years of my life. That whole time, Kayla, you were enthralled with my voice. I softly whispered that one of the most important things in my life was for you to know how much I loved you. For you see, Kayla, if I impress all the people in the world, but fail to have an impact on you, I have failed. I

88

ended our walk by praying for you. I prayed that you might know how deep and great is your Heavenly Father's love for you. If there were one thing in the world I would want you to know in your life, it would be this: The love that I have for you comes from Jesus, Kayla. He has been and always will be the greatest love of my life. I live solely because of His love for me. If you know me as well as you do now and I have not communicated that to you, I have greatly erred. After our first adventure that night, I came back inside, cradled you in my arms, and sang you this song, our song, Kayla.

> Close to You
> Why do birds suddenly appear, every time you draw near?
> Just like me they long to be close to you.
> Why do stars fall down from the sky
> Every time you walk by?
> Just like me, they long to be
> Close to you.
>
> On the day that you were born the angels got together and decided to
> Create a dream come true,
> So they sprinkled gold mist in your hair and golden starlight in your eyes of blue.
> That is why all the guys in town
> Follow you all around
> Just like me they long to be—Close to you.
> (The Carpenters)

You stared into my eyes for the entire song, and then slowly faded into the place where dreams come true. While you slept, I watched you, cried, and prayed for the gift from heaven wrapped up as my Kayla. And that, Kayla, was the day we bonded.

I love you and Happy Birthday…
Love, Aunt Kristi

# How You've Grown

By Michael & Kristi Powers

It is with great pleasure that Kristi and I wish our niece Jennifer a happy seventeenth birthday today.

For those of you who aren't familiar with Jennifer Pozanni, she is an All-State basketball player in Wisconsin, who is a junior at Beloit Memorial High School. Jen led the Rock Valley Conference in scoring as a freshman and sophomore, and then after transferring to Beloit Memorial her junior year, led the Big Eight Conference in scoring, and was the All-Area Player of the Year. She is by far the best girl's basketball player I have ever seen.

To top all that off, she is also the most humble and team-orientated player a coach could ever hope to have. While the spotlight has been on her in the media the entire year, she has praised and brought attention to her teammates in every newspaper article. She learned at an early age that the sound carries twice as far if you let someone else talk about you, so Jen, WE are blowing the horn this morning, and the sound is literally going throughout the world.

We love you, and want you to know that we are so proud of you...
Happy Seventeenth Birthday,
Michael and Kristi

How You've Grown

(Written from Kristi's perspective)


Dear Jennifer,

Wow... seventeen already... Where has the time gone?

I vividly remember you as a five-year-old, and I knew then that you would be a great athlete. You had the most muscular legs I have ever seen in a young child. Even at that age, you were better than the boys at any game.

It has been a joy to have you in our family, and I cannot imagine our lives without you. In just one short year you will sprout wings and fly away from the nest. While we will be happy for you, we will also cry, as a chapter of our life will be through. We want you to know how much we love and care for you, Jen. If we were to influence all the young women that Michael has coached, and yet not influenced you, our niece, then we have failed you. What I want to share with you on this, your seventeenth birthday, is something that has been in my mind and heart for a long time.

I have thought about how much life is like your last basketball game this past season. The game had every emotion. I wanted so much to catch your eye at the beginning of the game and tell you these words, "Remember this feeling, Jen! Keep this feeling close to your heart and remember it always!" I wanted you to remember the thrill of arriving on the bus over an hour before it started and seeing the streams of people flocking to the gym. I wanted you to remember the joy of running into the gym, your team by your side, to a standing-room-only crowd. I wanted you to remember the nervous feeling in your stomach at the sound of the buzzer as the twenty-minute warm-up ended, and to embrace the memory of the roar of the crowd, a roar so loud that you were not sure if that really was your name being called for the starting line-up. How about playing a team that was ranked 17th in the nation and knowing that victory was within your grasp at half-time when the score was almost tied? How about the incredible feeling as you looked up in the stands and saw your little sister and brother holding a sign that said how proud they were of you? Or the love you experienced by knowing that you had at least twenty-five family members there to root just for you? One of the most precious moments to me was at the end of the game. Although it was not a victory, I cried inside as your eight-year-old brother, Jordan, got your attention at the end of the game and said "Good game, Jen," in the way only Jordan can.

All those feelings are wonderful, Jen, but there was one Person there that you did not see. In fact He cares more for you than all the loved ones that were there combined. HE was sitting in the stands, too. HE is the One who will be with you all your life. HE will be the one who cheers the loudest when you win in life, and cries the hardest when you face defeat. And HE will be the one who takes your hand and guides you to which path you should choose when you start your adult life next year. The unseen Guest of course is Jesus. If you should never step on another basketball court again, remember that day, Jen, and remember your biggest Fan who loves you...

We leave you with a song entitled: "How You've Grown" by Natalie Merchant. Kristi and I both sit here with tears in our eyes as we listen to the song and write this tribute to you.

How You've Grown

"My how you've grown." I remember that phrase from my childhood days too.
"Just wait and see." I remember those words and how they chided me.
When patient was the hardest thing to be.
Because we can't make up for the time that we've lost, I must let these memories provide. No little girl can stop her world to wait for me.
I should have known. At your age, in a string of days the year is gone.
But in that space of time, it takes so long.

Because we can't make up for the time that we've lost, I must let these memories provide. No little girl can stop her world to wait for me.
Every time we say goodbye you're frozen in my mind as
the child that you never will be, you never will be again.
I'll never be more to you than a stranger could be.

Every time we say good-bye you're frozen in my mind as
the child that you never will be, will be again.

Happy Seventeenth birthday, Jen.

Your other biggest fans,
Kristi and Michael

# The King of Turtle Greens

I came across a letter I wrote to my son Caleb five years ago in one of my notebooks. This was about three years before I actually started writing seriously, but I had so many emotions inside me at the time, that I sat down at about 1:00 AM in the morning and wrote the following letter to Caleb after his Grandpa Conway died. Caleb was only a year and half old at the time and I figured he wouldn't remember much about his Grandpa...but I wanted to make sure he would never forget...

My Dearest Caleb,

As you grow older you are probably going to forget about Grandpa Conway. When you are old enough to read and understand this, I will give this letter to you...

I want you to remember...

Above everything else your grandpa loved you dearly. He was always very gentle with you and gave you lots of hugs and kisses.

I want you to remember...

That your grandpa liked to place you on his lap while he read your children's books. He was always very patient with you.

I want you to remember...

That grandpa was very, very concerned about your safety while you were at his house. He was so careful that he drove grandma crazy some times.

I want you to remember...

That your grandpa looked forward to teaching you how to play his favorite past-time: GOLF. First you would have received a "play" golf set. I put play in quotes because to grandpa, there was no such thing as a play golf set. All golf sets were serious! Then he would have had you putting the ball into grandma's drinking glasses in the living room. You would have graduated from there to going outside in the back yard and hitting the ball around. You would've had to
be very careful about hitting the ball into Farmer Gary's bean field though. Just ask your cousin Jordan about "hurting" Gary's beans. Finally he would have taken you on the ultimate golfing experience: A trip to the world famous Turtle Greens golf course run by Chuck and Linda Lucas just outside of Clinton, Wisconsin.

Now grandpa was a very good golfer, but that's not why everyone loved him there. No, they loved him because he was a real person. He was always friendly, considerate, and helpful. In fact, he was even patient enough to try and teach a volleyball player how to golf a couple of times. Yes, sir, Caleb, your grandpa Conway was well-loved by everyone he knew, but especially by those he met at Turtle Greens. He was not the best golfer there, but at Turtle Greens
he was king...

I want you to remember...

That your grandpa loved your mommy very much. He even gave her a nickname that sticks with her today: "Noodles." And nobody could say "Krissy" with more love and affection than him. Your grandpa was the one who gave me his blessing and permission to marry your mommy. I will tell you that story someday... It was the longest afternoon of my life!

I want you to remember...

That your grandpa was very kind and giving to me. I experienced many things in my life because he cared enough to include me in them. I remember duck hunting with him and experienced the most breathtaking sunrise filled with innumerable shades of orange and red, only to have my attention stolen by huge flocks of mallards as they appeared out of the painted mist that slowly rose from the surface of the water on the mighty Mississippi. We might not have said a word to each other as the sun slowly peeked her head over the misty water, but I have never felt closer to him than I did on those trips. He also took me Musky fishing in Northern Wisconsin a time or two. Although I didn't land one with him, I had the big one that got away on my line.

I want you to remember...

Your grandpa's sense of humor. He was a lot like your "Uncle Steve," in that he was funny even when he didn't know it. There are hundreds of Grandpa Conway stories we will tell you someday...

I want you to remember...

That your grandpa loved his family. Especially Grandma. It is hard to find two people who were more in love with each other than your grandparents. They were great role-models for your Mommy and Daddy to follow.

I want you to remember...

That your Grandpa had a soft spot for animals. Grandma always said, "Never marry a man who isn't kind to animals." Your Grandpa would sneak outside in the winter and make sure that "Momma Kitty", the country stray, was warm and fed. He was always being gruff about the animals when people were around, but when he thought they weren't looking, he was an old softy.

I want you to remember...

That your grandpa loved football. He even played semiprofessional football for the Delavan Red-Raiders. He would have taught you a lot about the game. I guess Uncle Rick and I will have to do that now. And Caleb, I don't say this lightly, but if you grew up to be a Green Bay Packer fan because of his influence, that would have made him very proud. And, although I won't admit this to anyone, it would have made me proud too...

Now if you grow up to be a Democrat...we might have some long discussions!

Most of all Caleb, I want you to remember...

That of all the people you will look up to in life, including me, Grandpa Conway would have been your role-model for the following things he taught me.

—Never Give Up

When Grandpa's first child was on the way he went down to the local General Motors plant and applied for a job but was told that they weren't hiring. Your grandpa went back every day for almost a month before they got so tired of his daily visits that they decided they did indeed have one opening. He retired from GM 28 years later and provided for his family by working hard...and never giving up.

—Honesty is the best policy.

—Love your family with all your heart.

—Be kind to animals. Especially when you think no one is looking.

—Enjoy God's Great Outdoors!

—Be a REAL person.

—Don't worry about what people may think of you. Do what's right.

—Give everyone an equal chance.

—Travel and see the world.

—Learn to play golf.

—Take lots of pictures of yourself.

—When you hear a Grizzly bear growl, run as fast as you can in the other direction, but don't turn your video camera off, so that your family can enjoy the moment with you later. (Actually Caleb, we know that you are not supposed to run from a bear, because he will think you are prey, but oh how we laughed after seeing his video!)

—Fear wild bears sometimes but don't fear the ones from Chicago.

—Don't ever let a kind word go unsaid.

Caleb, there is a whole "world" out there that you might not experience now that your Grandpa is gone. I know my life would be drastically different if your Grandpa had not been in my life, but I will try my best to teach you the life lessons and do the things that grandpa would have done with you. Whenever you hear a duck call, or a goose honk, think of your Grandpa Conway.

And God said, "Let the water teem with living creatures, and let the birds fly above the earth across the expanse of the sky." Genesis 1:20

Grandpa loves you...and I do too.

Daddy

*****

**Caleb Short Take**

It is that time of the year when earwigs find their way into our house. Our three-year-old, Caleb, has watched his mommy wage war on the little buggers this last week, and yesterday he decided to help her out with the problem. He came from the bathroom, his face beaming with pride, and said, "Mommy, there was an earwig in the bathroom, so I took your shoe and killed it. Then I threw it in the toilet, then I peed on it, and then I flushed it down the toilet."

Bug control, Caleb style!

# Celebrating Life

One of my favorite quotes is: "Life is what happens while we make other plans."

I have known this for a number of years, but I still get caught up in the rat race.

"If only we had that bill paid off, then I could relax and enjoy life...If only I could quit my job at the post office and just do my video business, then I'd be happy...If only we could find a house in the country, with woods, rolling hills, and a stream."

And the goals seem to always be out of my reach...

I tend to put on blinders, focus on MY goals, forget that God has a plan for my life, and then miss out on all the things I should be taking the time to do. All the while, life is passing me by, my kids are growing up, and my wife is yearning for me to spend quality time with her...

Life is not about the perfect job, the big promotion, the car or house we just have to have. No, it is about all the little things that we pass up and just don't have the time to do while we strain so hard to reach our goals.

It's time to stop working 60-70 hour workweeks, learn to live within our means, and then start prioritizing our lives. It's time to drop everything and run out into the pouring rain with my three-year-old during a warm summer storm. It's time to pull over to the side of the road and watch the deer feeding in the meadow with her fawn. It's time to lie on our backs in the grass and see animal shapes in the white puffy clouds that float lazily by. It's time to stop talking about that family vacation and actually take it. It is time to stop telling our kids, "Not now, maybe later."

The later is now...It's time to start celebrating life!

# A Father's Love

His name was Brian, and he was a student at the small high school I attended. Brian was a special education student who was constantly searching for love and attention, but it usually came for the wrong reasons. Students who wanted to have some "fun" would ask, "Brian, are you the Incredible Hulk?" He would then run down the halls roaring and flexing. He was the joke of the school and was "entertainment" for those who watched. Brian, who was looking for acceptance, didn't realize that they were laughing at him and not with him. One day I couldn't take it anymore. I told the other students that I had had enough of their game and to knock it off. "Aw, come on, Mike! We are just having fun. Who do you think you are anyway?"

The teasing didn't stop for long, but Brian latched onto me that day. I had stuck up for him, and now he was my buddy. Thoughts of "What will people think of you if you are friends with Brian," swirled in my head, but I forced them out as I realized that God wanted me to treat this young man as I would want to be treated.

Later that week I invited Brian over to my house to play video games. We sat there playing Intellivision (this was the 80's) and drinking Tang. Pretty soon he started asking me questions like, "Hey Mike. Where do you go to church?" I would politely answer his questions, then turn my concentration back to the video games...He kept asking me questions about God, and why I was different from some of the kids at school. Finally my future wife, Kristi, who was my high school sweetheart at the time, pulled me aside and said, "Michael, he needs to talk. How about you go down to your room where you can talk privately?" My wonderfully perceptive girlfriend had picked up on the cues better than I had.

As soon as we arrived in my room, Brian asked again, "Hey, Mike. How come you're not like some of the other kids at school?" I knew I needed to tell him about the difference that God had made in my life. I got out my Bible and shared John 3:16 and some verses in Romans with him. I explained that God loved him just the way he was and that He had sent Jesus down to earth to die on a cross, rise from the dead, and make it possible for everyone, especially Brian, to spend eternity in heaven if they believed. I didn't know if he was comprehending what I was telling him, but when I finished explaining, I asked Brian if he wanted to pray with me. He said he would like that.

We prayed together: "God, I know I am a sinner, and that even if I were the only person on earth, You still would have sent Your Son down to die on the cross for me and take my place. I accept the gift of salvation that You offer, and I ask that You come into my heart and take control. Thank you, Lord. Amen."

I looked at him and said, "Brian, if you meant those words you just prayed, where is Jesus right now?"

He pointed to his heart and said, "He's in here now."

Then he did something I will never forget as long as I live. Brian hugged the Bible to his chest, lay down on the bed and let the tears flow down the side of his cheeks. When I cry, my sobbing is very loud, but Brian's was unearthly silent as the emotions he'd held inside let loose. Then he said to me, "Mike, do you know that the love that God has for me must be like the love a husband has for his wife?"

I was floored.

Here was someone who had trouble comprehending things in school, but had now understood one of eternity's great truths. I knew now that he understood what I had shared with him.

He lay there for another five minutes or so as the salty drops continued to flow.

I still remember the incredible feeling I had at that moment: a high higher than anything a substance could ever give—the high of knowing that God still works miracles in everyday life. John 10:10 immediately came to mind: "...I have come that they may have life, and have it to the full."

It was about a week later that everything came into perspective for me. It was then that Brian really opened up to me. He explained that his dad had left him and his mom when he was five years old. As Brian stood on the porch that day, his dad told him he was leaving because he couldn't deal with having a son like him anymore. Then he walked out of Brian's life and was never seen again... Brian told me that he had been looking for his dad ever since. Now I knew why the tears kept flowing that day in my bedroom. His search was over. He found what he had been looking for since he was five years old...

A Father's Love...

# The Diploma

I was exhausted from working my two jobs over the weekend and was not looking forward to the graduation ceremony. I have been to many graduations and I know how boring they are for most people. To top everything off, my wife and I had our two kids under the age of three with us. Both of the kids were squirming and whining, and I knew it was going to be a long afternoon. Our sole comic relief came when my three-year-old patted and rubbed the head of a bald man we did not know in front of us. As the ceremony dragged on I kept thinking of all the places I would rather be, and made up my mind that I wasn't going to enjoy myself.

It was your ordinary graduation ceremony: a hot, sweaty auditorium filled with people fanning themselves with their programs, listening to speech upon boring speech, and the endless calling of names as each matriculator walked across the stage to grab this piece of paper that symbolized his or her academic accomplishment. It was getting harder and harder to pay attention. Just as my attitude started to go sour, they began calling out the graduate's names. The classmates formed a single file line and made their way up towards the podium.

That's when I caught my first close-up glimpse of Kim. She looked up at us and was trying in vain to hold back the tears. She was not doing a good job of it. Believe me, holding back emotions is not something that Kim does very well. There she was, standing in line, about to receive her diploma, and she was probably thinking about a number of things. Maybe her dad who passed away a few years ago and didn't get to see her reach her goal, or her grandmother, who also passed away recently, and who had always wanted to attend college, but her family didn't have the money...

For me it was like something from a movie. You know, the dramatic slow motion scene where all the crowd noise grows quiet, and the camera slowly moves up on her face as the tears begin to fall. She was a good distance away from us, but to me it was as if she were standing in front of me. That simple act of looking up at those loved ones who had come to watch her graduate, and gently rubbing the tears of joy, accomplishment, and pride out of her eyes really got through to me. The selfishness in me melted away, and I realized why I was there and not somewhere else.

"KIMBERLY ANNE CONWAY, GRADUATING MAGNA CUM LAUDE," came booming over the auditorium's sound system, and she walked gracefully across the huge stage and received this piece of paper that symbolized so many things to her. Then just before she walked off the stage, she turned around towards those who had come to share the day with her, and, with the brightest smile on her face, waved and grinned at us like a little girl getting on the school bus for the first time.

I glanced at my wife, and saw the tear-drops roll gently down as the love she had for her sister manifested itself on her face.

You see, Kim is not your ordinary college graduate. She is thirty-eight years old, and has stuck with her goal of graduating from college for the past twenty years. It's not like she is going to look back on that part of her life, sigh, and say, "College...the best twenty years of my life!"

She attended college while working full time, and she studied extremely hard, especially the past couple of years as she pushed toward her goal of a college degree. Many times she felt like quitting, and, if it weren't for her support group of other nontraditional students that cared for her, she would have given up on her goal. Many times she would call one of the other students she knew and tell them she wanted to quit, and would be talked out of it. Then a while later this student would call her and say she wanted to quit and Kim would talk her out of it...(Luckily, they both didn't want to quit at the same time!)

I have the utmost respect for Kim. It takes a special person to stick with a goal as long as she has. I attended college for three years when I got out of high school, but I stopped when I wasn't sure what I wanted to do with my life. Many times I have looked back and wished that I had stuck with it and gone on to be a high school teacher. If for no other reason, I wish I had finished something that I had started.

I know what it feels like to walk out of that last final exam of the semester, breathe in the fresh air just outside the doors of the university, and feel like the weight of the world has been lifted off your shoulders for at least a little while. I can't even begin to imagine what it felt like for Kim after so many years...

I love you, Kim, and I want you to know that I admire you for that symbolic piece of paper that will soon adorn a wall in your house.

In the words of Caleb, my three-year-old: "HAPPY GRADULATION, AUNT KIMMY!"

\*\*\*\*\*

## Caleb Short Take

One year we came back from camping exhausted, but with some great memories. Little did we know that there was one more memory yet to be experienced.

On that particular trip, Caleb had to learn not to throw empty wrappers and cans into the lake. It only took one talk about littering, and what it does to nature, to convince him not to do it. The day we got back, Kristi happened to look out the window into the back yard, and, to her horror, she saw that Caleb was going to the bathroom on our lawn. Now, being a guy, I didn't think this was too big a problem until I found out that the two young neighbor kids were watching him...and that he wasn't going "number one", as we say; he was going "number two." (When I was his age, we called it going "Brown Crayon." Yes, I was a little weird growing up.) When Caleb was done doing his business, Kristi called him into the house and explained to him that when he is camping and there are no toilets, he can go potty outside, but when he is home, he has to come inside and go in the toilet. As she went on with her lecture, he began to hang his head as he just didn't quite grasp the concept. She could just hear the wheels turning in his head: Why was it okay to do it yesterday, but not today? Finally the light bulb went on over his head!

"Awwwww Mommy...When I go potty in the back yard, is that called littering?!"

# Memory Lane

**By Kristi Powers**

One morning, when I was twenty-two years old, I jumped out of bed and ran to the window to gaze out over "The Lane," as I called it. I loved everything about my walks down this special path, for my journeys were full of beauty, solitude, and communion with my Maker. This particular morning, as the sun peeked her head over the horizon, I was overcome with emotion and memories...

I had a favorite Calico cat named Missy, who was my constant companion. More than anything, we shared a love for taking strolls down The Lane. I would gently pick her up, and she would make her way up to my shoulders to wrap herself around the back of my neck. Oh, how I loved those beautiful summer days, feeling the lush soft grass under my bare feet and my patchwork-quilt companion around my neck. I would often pause and gaze up ahead as we started our journey. My eyes would follow The Lane as it stretched downward toward the bottom of the field. From there it climbed steadily until it gradually disappeared on the horizon.

To one side of The Lane stood a field of corn, and there were many times that the wind would blow and rustle the leaves of the stalks as we walked by, as if to applaud our coming. Adjacent to the cornfield was a pasture full of horses who quietly nickered their "hello" to us as we sauntered by. Halfway down the path stood my favorite tree, an old massive oak that I named the "fireplace tree," for the bottom of the trunk was hollowed out in the shape of a hearth. When I was very young, I would leave letters inside of the tree, thinking they would stay there forever and that someday, when I was older, I would come back to read them.

From there, the Lane climbed steadily upward to an old bladeless windmill with a rusted-out, but functional, pump underneath it. "The

Tower," as I called it, seemed to be a monument that marked this place as special.

There was something so holy about where The Lane led and the atmosphere surrounding it. As we stood on the top of this knoll, we could see for miles around to all the neighboring fields and woods, and I would pause to hear God's whisper in the gentle fluttering of the trees. I often felt as if we were on the top of the world overlooking all creation, and it was here that I would sit down and carry on serious discussions with my Creator. Many times the wind would blow gently across my face and I always believed it to be the kind hand of God caressing my cheek.

I recall the Angora-soft milkweed that grew near the tower in the fall. I would make a wish, blow the fluffy seeds into the wind, and watch them gently float away.

In the winter it became my family's sledding hill. We even had nighttime toboggan rides as we were pulled behind our neighbor's tractor, often times harmonizing our voices in song, as the full moon would light our way. I can still see the faces of my neighbors, parents, and siblings as the moonbeams created glowing silhouettes against the pure white snow.

In the spring, I remember the freshly-plowed fields with their deep rich earth smell, and the dandelions as they burst open and dotted the landscape with yellow...

I slowly came back to the present and took one last look at The Lane. The skyline still held a pink tint where the sun had just risen. The mist gathered from the floor of the pathway, swirled upwards, and disappeared. In my mind's eye, I could see her—the little blond-haired girl with the patchwork-quilt cat draped around her neck. She was smiling at me as she stopped and waved. And then, just as the vapor slowly gathered and disappeared, so did my image of her. I mouthed the words, "Good-bye," choked back my emotions, and stooped to gather the delicate, white lace bridal gown in my arms. It was only then that I noticed my mother had been watching me. I looked at her through my tear-filled eyes, and she tenderly returned my gaze. Finally, she turned away to hide her tears, and said in a low voice, "See you at the church."

# Do We Take the Dogs?

It all started with the big decision. Do we take our dogs camping with us? Kristi said, "Yes!" and I said, "Definitely not!" Kristi wanted to take the dogs because I like to disappear for hours on end hiking, fishing and exploring, and she wanted to be able to take the dogs for walks during these times so that she felt safe. I said the dogs would be too much trouble and hassle...We took the dogs.

Our first day in the Nicolet National Forest in Northern Wisconsin went well as we set up camp and got situated. We enjoyed sitting around the campfire until we got tired, and then we went off to sleep in our tent. Around 2:00 a.m. one of our dogs started scratching at the tent door. Kristi let her out, thinking she was heeding the call of nature. About twenty seconds after she went out she came flying back into the tent, whining and rolling around on everything, including us. At the same time this incredibly overpowering smell assaulted us! Not only did we find it hard to breathe, but our eyes turned to water instantly. Those who have smelled a skunk along the highway have no idea what sniffing our wild and odiferous friend is like up close and personal. It was like having ammonia poured over our heads! I am a very, very, sound sleeper, and I slowly came to my senses...my sense of smell first! Kristi said, "I think she got sprayed by a skunk!"

While we discussed if it were indeed a skunk or if some evil entity had taken possession of our beloved pet, our dog was rolling all over us, our clothes, and our sleeping bags in her attempt to get her eyes to stop burning. Needless to say Kristi and I and our other dog went piling out of the tent as fast as we could. Both our dogs are females, and I usually let ladies go first, but this was one time I was glad for my athletic ability, as I was the first to stumble out into the fresh air.

Now, being the incredibly sensitive and mature husband that I was at the age of twenty-two, the first words out of my mouth were, "Kristi! I told you we should have never taken the dogs with us! I knew something like this was going to happen! Why didn't you listen to me!"

After I got over my childish outburst, we decided that the best thing to do was to take the air mattress out of the tent, put it near the campfire and try to salvage what was left of a good night's sleep. There was absolutely no way we were going to go back into the tent...

I finally fell asleep again, but Kristi was having a hard time sleeping, mostly because of the way I made her feel...Just as she was drifting off, she heard a familiar noise, but couldn't place it. She heard what sounded like hundreds of people clapping from a long distance away, but the clapping started getting closer...Finally she realized it was the sound of very heavy rain as it moved its way across the forest. She woke me up and said, "Michael, we are about to get very wet."

I could hear the rain getting closer, and, when we could hear the droplets hit the other side of Bear Lake and start to make their way to our campsite, we had to make a decision. Do we stay put and get soaked to the bone, or do we climb back into the tent of horrors?! Our decision was made for us when we began to be pelted by huge drops of cold, stinging water. We decided to climb back into the tent. In we went, all four of us. Seconds later, out went a very bad smelling dog. It was unbearable to be in an enclosed area with her. Our poor dog was so afraid of being paid another visit from her striped friend that she was frantically trying to get back into the tent, and I had to go back out into the downpour to tie her up to a tree...Hey, call PETA if you want to, but there was no way we were going to be anywhere near that dog. We spent a cold, stinky, miserable night.

The next morning was spent surveying the damage and salvaging what clothes and materials we could. Kristi went to the nearest town, about thirty minutes away, bought some tomato juice and washed all of our clothes at a Laundromat. I spent the day pouring tomato juice over the dog, rubbing it in, and then throwing her into the lake to wash it off. I repeated the process about ten times. Before long, my dog wouldn't even come near me. Tomato juice helped, but in no way took even half the smell away. We spent another smelly night, but this one went by without incident. We were awakened the next morning about 5:30 a.m. to the sound of a person saying, "Whewwww! You guys stink!!!!"

The night before, we had phoned our friends, Steve and Sarah, who were going to be camping with us for the rest of the week, and explained what had happened, but nothing had prepared them for what they smelled.

We went on to enjoy the rest of our camping trip, but I do have to admit that towards the end of the week, (and I'm not proud of this) I wore my wife's underwear. I didn't bring enough to last the week.

There. It's out. Michael wore women's underwear. Deal with it.

I know some of you are sitting there saying, "Why in the world would anybody want to go camping?" Besides the obvious advantages of getting away from it all and enjoying God's creation, there is something about camping that brings people closer together. Yes, things always go wrong, and there is always that moment when we stop and think, "Why are we doing this?" I obviously didn't handle this situation very well, but it is something that we have laughed about for the past eight years. When we talk about the trip, the conversation is like this: "Remember when you did that?...Oh yeah, and then you did..." And the conversation goes on as we laugh and tell our favorite camping stories.

Camping brings a family closer together. I'm convinced of it. In fact one of our favorite authors, Gary Smalley, has done research on families that he has come across that are genuinely close and loving to each other. One of the things they had in common was that they all were camping families! Now obviously, it is not the only way a family can grow closer, and I'm not saying that it is the cure-all, but I am saying that our family has grown closer together because we camp.

As we head north this week, I look forward to camping equipment flying off the top of our car, flat tires, five hours in the car with our little ones, insect bites, rain dripping through the tent, fishing hooks getting stuck in our ears, raccoons getting into our food, and screaming kids...

Yes, all the ingredients needed to bring a family closer together.

I just have to keep Caleb away from the skunks!

# Teo's Quest

"Hey Teo! (pronounced Tay-O) When are you going to learn how to do this sort?" teased one of my co-workers at the USPS Processing and Distribution Center where I work third shift. Teofil let out a hearty laugh as he walked in circles looking for the correct route number on which to place the tub of mail that he had in his hand.

"You really ought to try working down here more often!" teased another. Teofil just smiled and laughed again, but continued to look for the right place. I walked up to him and asked which town he had. He told me and I showed him the route it went to. "Don't worry Teofil, it just takes a while to learn this sort. You'll get the hang of it before long," I told him. "And pay no attention to the teasing. They are just having some fun with you. All of us had to start learning at one point or another."

"I really should know how to do this sort by now, though," he confided to me in his heavy Romanian accent when the co-workers left the work area. "I have trouble remembering things since I was in prison in Romania." My mouth dropped open. "They used to put a drug in our tea every morning, and I have trouble with my short-term memory now— bromium, I think it was."

Over the next couple of weeks he opened up and told me his incredible story.

Teofil Dursina and his future wife, Carolina, lived in Communist Romania in 1987, but they wanted to escape the country and come to America. They were given a map of the border which showed the best places to attempt a crossing and set off with a friend in the twenty degrees below zero weather to try to make their way to freedom. Things didn't go exactly as planned, and sixty miles and three days later, they were hopelessly lost. The third night they kept walking, on the lookout for booby traps, barbed wire, electric fences, and border guards who were instructed to shoot to kill. How one was treated when caught all depended on how close to the border they were captured. They stopped only to eat snow to quench their thirst, having run out of their meager food and water supplies earlier in the day.

109

The next morning they were spotted by some Romanian farmers and were turned in.

Romanian citizens who lived near the border were monetarily rewarded for turning in those who were illegally trying to cross the border. The border guards were given extra money, rations, and time off for capturing people trying to make their way to freedom.

They were beaten, handcuffed, and then taken to a border base where they were strip-searched and questioned. They were not allowed to sleep and were given no food or water for the entire day.

From this base they were sent to a larger military base where they were strip-searched again, beaten, and interrogated all night long. The three of them were separated into different rooms. When questioned, they were beaten periodically after certain answers and were told that what they said did not match the stories of the other two, even when telling the truth. All three were forced to stand all night long, again with no food, no water, and no sleep. Half-way through the night, German shepherds were used as part of the interrogation. If they didn't answer the way the guards wanted them to, the dogs were turned loose on them. After Teo continued to pass out, the interrogation stopped for a few hours.

Later that morning they were handcuffed, chained, and hauled to Oravita Army Base. Here they were questioned by Romanian Intelligence for two days and were given a chunk of bread and cup of water once each day. Throughout this two-day interrogation, they had electric shock applied to the base of their skulls, and were beaten with billy clubs and rubber hoses until they lost consciousness.

They were then brought with no legal representation before a judge in Oravita, and falsely accused of numerous crimes besides the illegal border crossing attempt. All three were sentenced to one year in prison.

Then they were taken to jail through the city streets in chains while people jeered and taunted them.

The three of them were separated in jail and were confined in six-by-six foot cells, seven people to a cell. The room contained bunk beds (they slept three to a bed), no light, and one barred window high above. The cell was never cleaned and the stench was overwhelming. Teofil spent a month in what he described as the worst part of his confinement.

The entire month they wore the same clothes that they had on when they were caught. The toilet for all seven of them was a bucket that was emptied once a day. After the first week they were allowed out of the room for five minutes a day. In the morning they were given a cup of tea that was laced with bromium which, among other things, had short and long term effects on his memory. While some periods of his life are still vividly entrenched in his memory, he has no recollection now of parts of his childhood and teenage years.

For food they were given half a slice of moldy bread, a bowl of hot water with two salad leaves, and some old fish that was leftover from the military base's food. Other times they would get boiled barley that would expand in their stomachs to make them feel full. Bugs and worms were constantly found in the food and huge rats made their way through the bars in the door to try and get at their food.

Each and every day of this seemingly eternal month, they were interrogated, with the guards having their "fun" beating the prisoners with metal tubes wrapped in rubber, clubs and fists. They were not allowed to shower or bathe and were given no clothes, underwear, or shoes. Teofil spent the entire thirty days in the same clothes.

Here was Teofil, twenty-two years old, having lived with his parents his entire life, now being thrust into a nightmare. Teofil's mom came to visit many times, bringing things to him. She was not allowed to see him, but the guards told her they would deliver the items to him. The items never reached him, as they were confiscated by the guards.

Teofil, Carolina, and their friend were then transferred to Timisoara Prison where they spent the next five months.

There, one hundred prisoners were confined together, two to a bed, with one toilet for all. Teofil made his body adjust to use the bathroom at night only, when there wasn't such a demand for the only "bathroom." He could never get used to sitting there while five others stood next to him waiting.

The inmates were separated into three groups: men, women, and juveniles. When the lights went out at night, Teofil could hear the women and juveniles brutally fighting each other. Surprisingly the women were more likely to be heard fighting than the men, and unmentionable things went on every night on the juvenile side...

Guards who were bored would amuse themselves every day by beating prisoners, and many of the inmates would mentally crack and go insane. Prison doctors and dentists would perform experimental surgery and pull teeth with no anesthesia and no painkillers afterwards. Teofil and the rest of the prisoners tried very hard to stay healthy so that they wouldn't have to go to either of them.

Small portions of food consisted of a half piece of bread, potatoes, beans, and the same drugged tea they had been given earlier in their confinement. Once a week, as a treat, they were given fatty meat full of gristle. Meals were served with no eating utensils in old aluminum bowls, and were shared by two people. Teofil learned not to complain about anything when a prisoner next to him had four teeth knocked out for complaining that he had to eat from the same bowl as someone who was extremely sick. The unfortunate inmate was given no dental assistance afterwards.

Prisoners were made to prepare food for the military camp that was next door, and would drool over the "delicacies" they handled but could not consume. When one inmate tried to smuggle an onion back to his cell, the guards found it on him, smashed it into his face, rubbed it in his eyes and then made him eat onion after onion until he vomited.

Finally the prisoners were given clothes to wear, and for the first time in weeks, Teofil could wear something different from what he had been captured in. However, the clothes were used, including the underwear, which they were able to change once a week. They were also issued fifteen-year-old boots that didn't fit. The only "luxury" they were given was a shower; that is, if groups of fifty or more in a room where cold water came out of the ceiling for three minutes can be called a shower.

Through it all, Teofil worried about Carolina, who was kept in another part of the prison. He never saw her the entire time he was there. They were able to keep sporadic contact through a unique courier service provided by those prisoners who had been there for years and were allowed to work in the prison, doing laundry or delivering food. Notes were passed via these unlikely messengers, but not very often for fear of being caught.

The prisoners were in constant fear of torture. They tried to do nothing that would catch the guards' attention in any way. If a guard didn't like them, or just felt particularly bored, they would pass the time by making life a literal hell for those unfortunate enough to be singled out.

Torture took on many forms. Inmates were tied to tables and beat until unconscious, revived with cold water and beaten again. Some were made to stand barefoot for hours at a time in a special room where salt water ran like a constant stream across the floor, wearing the flesh off their feet.

Other torture included confinement in total darkness for up to three months and then being brought out into the sunlight. Prisoners would also be chained to a wall spread-eagle and given only water until they were so weak they just hung from the chains.

Teofil was then transferred to a prison in Bucharest for a month and then was sent on to one in Codlea.

A few days after being transferred to the prison in Codlea, an alarm sounded and all the prisoners dropped to the floor immediately. Teofil had no idea what was going on, but figured he had better drop to the floor also. He found out that those who didn't were beaten. This alarm meant that someone had just been executed. Inmates would be removed from their rooms, stripped naked and made to run down a cement corridor that was hundreds of yards long. They were told if they made it to the other side, they would be allowed to go back to their confinement, but they were always shot somewhere in the corridor. Fellow prisoners were made to collect the bodies, clean the mess out of the corridor, and bury the corpses in the fields outside of the prison. Families of the executed were not informed, and to this day there is no record of how many prisoners are buried there.

Many times prisoners were told they would be released in a week or so, only to have the deadline come and go, along with their hope of being free, so when Teofil was told he would be released in two weeks, he didn't believe it. "They are just playing with my head," he told himself.

But he was released! HE WAS FINALLY FREE!

Teofil gradually made his way home, one painful step after another, and it took over a month to recover enough physically to even walk fast. In fact, a few weeks after his release, he was attempting to play soccer with some friends. When he tried to run for the first time, he fell flat on his face. The muscles of his legs had atrophied so much in his confinement that they couldn't support him.

It was shameful to be in prison for any reason in Romania, and Teofil struggled with the thought of returning home and facing his parents. By the time he arrived, Teofil felt clean inside, refusing to feel shame for trying to escape to freedom.

He was lovingly accepted back into the family with a great many hugs and tears, but it was bittersweet, as he still didn't know what had become of his Carolina. He contacted her parents and was told that they had not received word about her. As the weeks went by, he became more and more anxious for the safety of his fiancée. Then about three weeks after he was released, his future wife walked into his home. She too had been released! He held her close and was afraid to let go for fear that he would lose her again. They shared what might have been the longest hug in the history of the world...

It took eight long months for Teofil to find a job as he was turned down many times due to his conviction. Gradually, Teofil and Carolina tried to get back to some sense of normalcy, but they never lost their desire to escape communist Romania and experience freedom.

It wasn't long before Teofil found himself wandering around the borders again, looking for a way to cross. When Teofil told me this, I said to him, "Are you crazy, Teo?! You tried to escape again, even after all you went through?!"

"Michael, you will never know what it feels like to live without your freedom. I knew the consequences when I first tried to escape, and I was more than willing to try it again."

His statement profoundly touched me and I realized how much I take my freedom herein the United States for granted.

Twice more Teofil tried to cross the border. The first time, he found himself lost in the wilderness near the border again. He spent three more cold nights searching for a way into Yugoslavia, but he realized he had no chance to make it and turned back.

A few months later he tried escaping into Hungary, on the other end of the country. Teofil and his cousin tried to jump from a train and make a mad dash to freedom. They took a deep breath, opened the train door and prepared to jump, but as soon as they poked their heads out the door, the train passed a guard who was stationed along the tracks. Overcoming the instant shock, the guard pumped a round of ammunition in the chamber and took aim at them. They scrambled back into the train, ran to their room, changed into other clothes they had brought with them for just such an incidence, and positioned themselves in the dining car, trying to make it look as if they weren't scared to death. They hurried off the train at the next city and made a mad dash to lose themselves in the crowds to avoid being caught.

Teofil and Carolina were finally married, but ironically they never did escape communist Romania. Rather they walked out of the country, hand in hand, on tourist passports when communism fell in 1989.

They spent time in Italy and Austria, learning Italian and German respectively, before they were finally able to obtain visas to come to the U.S. Eventually they taught themselves English by watching TV while they lived in New York! Who says that TV is bad for you!

They finally settled down in Wisconsin where Teofil was able to obtain a job with the postal service, where he presently works.

I recently asked Teofil if he was angry about the eight months of his life, not to mention the parts of his memory, that were taken away from him. Without pausing, he responded, "No. I was aware of the possible consequences when I tried to escape." I interrupted him and said, "Teofil, if that happened to me, I would be so angry for the part of my life that was 'wasted' while I sat in prison."

He tilted his head to the side, looked me straight in the eye, and answered, "I do not regret it in the least bit. There is nothing in this life now that will ever make me worry. Nothing fazes me now that I have gone through that. Things that bother most people only make me laugh now. I have my Carolina and my freedom. What more could I possibly want?"

I can't even begin to explain how those words have affected me...

Teofil has given me a new outlook on a number of things. I have a newfound appreciation for the great country that I live in. I have to say that I have taken my freedom for granted.

I will also think twice before I complain about my inconsequential day-to-day problems, as I can't even imagine going through what Teofil and Carolina went through. I have a tremendous amount of respect for the lack of bitterness that Teofil shows through it all. I honestly think that I wouldn't have the same outlook if I were thrust into the same situation.

Most of all, I will think twice before I judge someone. We never know what a person has dealt with in his or her life. What seems so obvious on the surface may not be the real reason for their unexplained actions. The reason Teofil was having trouble learning the job operation was not because he was unintelligent or lazy, but because of circumstances that were beyond his control. As horrible as those circumstances were, they caused him to become a better person.

There are people in my life that I judge every day and I can't understand why they act the way they do...

Maybe there is more to their stories also...

# Thoughts on Turning Thirty

I have had mixed feeling about turning thirty. As an athlete I started thinking my prime competitive years were over and that I would have to get used to the idea that I am not going to be able to keep competing at a high level for too much longer. When people turn thirty, they also naturally start to look at their life and think about what they have accomplished and not accomplished so far. What do I have to show for myself? Am I a success? Do I have any regrets?

As my twenty-ninth year of life came to a close, I started thinking more and more about leaving my twenties behind and entering a new era in my life. Quite frankly, I was not looking forward to it.

A couple of weeks before my birthday, Darla Monroe, the mother of one of the basketball players I coach, let me know that she was going to have a surprise birthday party for her daughter Kristin's eighteenth birthday. As soon as I found out, I thought, "We have got to do a video of Kristin's life for her party."

Her mom was thinking the same thing, so she and her husband, Bill, brought me pictures and videotapes of Kristin growing up. I put together a video of her life and couldn't wait until the party to show it to her.

Kristin is a very special young lady to me and to lots of other people, and I just kept thinking how wonderful it was that her parents were going to all this trouble for her birthday to show her how much she meant to everyone. Thoughts of me turning thirty went on the back burner as my energy went to making Kristin's day special.

The weekend approached...

My wife Kristi asked me what I wanted to do for my birthday on Sunday. Kristin's party was on Saturday and after that I had a ton of other video editing that needed to be done. However, I knew I'd have to agree to do something on Sunday, even though I wasn't crazy about turning thirty!

Saturday came and I couldn't wait to surprise Kristin! We arrived at the Tiffany Inn a little after 5:00 p.m., and I had to get one last TV set up to show her video. I was chomping at the bit. Kristin and her parents were scheduled to get there sometime between 5:15 and 5:30, and I couldn't wait to get inside and get the video ready to play, so I grabbed the TV out of the trunk and I walked inside...

"SURPRISE!!!!!!!!"

I thought to myself, "Ha, ha, very funny." Either everyone was kidding with me, pretending I was Kristin, or they were just practicing for when she walked in the doors. I quickly glanced to one side of the room, half smiled and mumbled, "Yeah whatever..." and I continued my quest to set up the TV on the table. I walked another seven steps or so before an image flashed into my mind. I saw my sister-in-law Kim, with her bright red sweatsuit and a big old smile on her face. Within a split second I had a bunch of thoughts go through my mind:

"Why is Kim here?"

She had stopped by my practice recently, so she must have seen Kristin in the other gym, and that's why she's here.

"No, dufus, seeing someone one time doesn't get you invited to a surprise party!"

"Did I really see Kim?"

(If not, I have to tell my wife that I am seeing visions of her sister!)

"This is not good."

(All right, Michael, I think there were some other people that shouldn't be here. You need to take another look.)

I slowly came to a stop just feet away from my destination, and I turned, TV in hand...

Yep! There was Kim, smiling from ear to ear. I went from face to face and saw family and friends all laughing loudly at me...I don't remember exactly what I said to everyone, but, boy, did I feel bad. I had walked in the doors and totally snubbed everyone who had come to surprise me. It had never occurred to me that people would be there for me also, and I was totally shocked. Speaking of shocked, my three-year-old son Caleb had walked in the door right behind me, and when everyone yelled surprise, he went flying back out the door, crying his eyes out. "Those people scared me Daddy!"

So here is the scene at the Tiffany Inn: Michael walks in the door; people who have taken valuable time out of their schedule come to surprise him for his birthday, and Michael walks on by hardly acknowledging them, and his son runs screaming and crying out the door! Talk about gratitude! Later I found out everyone thought I had found out about the surprise and was being arrogant about it. Boy, did I feel bad about it and I spent the next five minutes trying to explain why I had behaved in such a manner.

Out of the corner of my eye I spotted two people whom I knew shouldn't have been there. I blinked and realized that they were for real. Carole and Bart, Caleb's grandpa and grandma on my wife's side, were there. How? They were supposed to be in Jekyll Island, Georgia, where they were spending most of the winter. Come to find out, Carole had found out about my party two days before, and they had hopped on a plane and flown back to Wisconsin! I was stunned. I couldn't believe they would do that. It meant more to me than they will ever know. (Now contrary to what others may tell you, the only reason they came back was to wish me a happy birthday. It had absolutely nothing, I repeat, absolutely nothing to do with missing all their grandchildren!)

I hurriedly started setting up the TV's to show Kristin's video before she and her family got there. Suddenly a thought occurred to me. "This is not right. I should not be a part of this. This is supposed to be Kristin's special day, and now the focus is going to be on me, too." I won't lie to you. It really started bothering me. There aren't many eighteen-year-old girls who would want to "share" a big day in their life with some thirty-year-old, over-the-hill, geek. I kept thinking, "This is all wrong!"

Before I could think it through, Kristin and her family arrived.

"SURPRISE!!!!"

Kristin walked in, shock registering on her face, and then she turned and buried her face in her mom and dad's shoulders. The tears came, and they shared a moment as she whispered words of thanks in their ears...

She walked around hugging and greeting everyone. The tears continued to flow, and I thanked God for being a part of it.

In a world that is so negative, so full of hate, despair and hopelessness, here was a young high school girl who was being shown how special she was, how much she was appreciated, how much her parents, family, and friends loved and supported her. I just could not keep from being encouraged and thinking how neat it was.

We started the video soon after and everyone got a chance to see Kristin grow up in about forty minutes, from infancy to her senior picture, and all the wonderful moments in between.

For those who don't know Kristin, she is a young lady who has been touched by something special her entire life. She competed in gymnastics, starting at an early age and going up to her freshman year in high school, winning numerous competitions. She ended her career with a trip to nationals in San Diego, where I believe she placed no lower than second place. Watching her tumbling in the floor routine reminded me so much of watching someone on ESPN. I couldn't believe how good she was. In junior high she won a basketball game on a last second shot, getting mobbed by her teammates and fans afterwards. She then gave up gymnastics to concentrate on her high school sports. In track she set school records, and earned a trip to State. In basketball she started on the varsity team as a freshman and blossomed into one of the best players on the team before blowing out her knee before her sophomore year. Dealing with this adversity is where I saw another side of her. She worked hard to rehab her knee and came back her junior year, only to re-injure it a couple of games into the season. I watched her deal with thinking she may never play competitive sports again. She worked hard again to rehab, but was told that she might not be able to play again...After sitting out two straight years of sports, she told her doctor that all she wanted was to play in one game her senior year. Just one game...My wife and I prayed that God might grant her one game... Well, she not only played in her one game, she played the entire season and was the Most Valuable Player! Oh yeah, I forgot to mention. She was the prom queen too!

But besides all the things that the world looks at as success, she has turned into one of the nicest Christian young ladies my wife and I have ever met. She carries herself with grace and class, and besides all she has going for her that could make her get stuck on herself, she has remained humble about the talents and gifts that God has given her. My prayer for her is that she continues to put God first in her life and allows Him take care of all the rest...

That evening she watched her first eighteen years go by, sharing the memories with her friends as they sat and laughed and cried...

I thought to myself, "This is how it should be," honoring someone and encouraging them in their young life." So often in our culture we only say nice things about someone after they have died. We all gather at a funeral and tell stories and good things about someone who can no longer hear them. Why do we do that? Why do we build someone up after they have gone into eternity? Why can't we do more things like this and tell people how much they mean to us when they are right there in front of us to be built up and encouraged?  We should celebrate life with the living, not just when they are gone...

I gave Kristin a hug after the video and told her how neat it was that her parents had pulled this all off for her. I then mentioned to her that I felt kind of uncomfortable sharing her day...She shut me right up and told me that she was very glad that she could share her birthday with me. That made me feel a lot better, but I still felt a twinge of guilt...

I then tried to mingle with everyone who had come and tell them how special it was to me that they were there. I was so touched. Here were people in my life who meant so much to me, and they had taken time out of their busy lives to wish me a happy birthday. My lovely wife then took me over to the corner of the room and showed me where they had set up a picture board of my life. Each picture had a caption, and right smack in the middle was a poem that my buddy Brian "Buzz" McGuigan had written about me. He roasted me pretty well through most of it, and I was touched again that he had taken the time to write it out. Slowly I started realizing that me being included wasn't a last second thing, but that it had been planned like this from the beginning...

Darla called Kristin and me over to the back of the room so we could get a picture with our cake...

The cake...

That was what finally broke the ice for me. It was a basketball cake with both our names on it. It finally hit me. This was planned this way from the beginning. I started getting emotional, but I was bound and determined not to cry in front of everyone. I was so humbled by the thought that her family thought enough of me to include me in their daughter's special day.

As I started opening presents, I laughed because most of the gifts were a kid's puzzle, coloring book, or something else that was a present for a child, not a thirty-year-old. The people who know me the best were giving me a hard time, because I refuse to grow up.

I started reading the cards, and again I had a hard time holding back the tears. I felt so loved, so appreciated. Besides the cards and gifts from everyone, Darla had two giant cards going around the room, one for each of us. On each one she had written something special, and then it went from person to person, as friends and family wrote a little something to us. When I started reading it, I couldn't hold back the salty drops from my eyes and I had to stop reading, or make a blubbering idiot of myself. I didn't read it again until I got home where I knew I could cry and cry and cry.

It frustrated me that I felt I couldn't spend enough time with each person who had come to see me. Each was special to me and I wanted to make sure I let everyone know how much I appreciated them, from my niece Jennifer, who hardly knew anyone there and probably could think of a thousand places she'd rather be (but it meant so much to me that she came anyway), to friends old and new. I especially appreciated seeing those couples who have played such a huge role in my life, men and women who have become our role models as examples of good marriages and the Christian walk. The only regret I have of the night is that I couldn't spend enough quality time with everyone.

As the night went on, and I was able to visit with friends I hadn't seen in a while, talk with former and current players of mine, and get to know some of Kristin's family I had not met, I felt more and more loved. I can honestly say that I didn't want to leave. The feeling that I had was indescribable. To think that God had blessed me with such wonderful friends and family was too much. I couldn't believe all the trouble that Darla, Bill, and my better half had gone through to make the night so special for Kristin and me. I was humbled by their actions.

As we got ready to leave, I tried to express to Darla and Bill how much it meant to me, but I just couldn't seem to find the right words...

Later in the car, on the way to visit with grandpa and grandma before they left again for Georgia, I told Kristi how much I loved her and appreciated her going through the trouble to surprise me. We talked as we drove along, and I started crying a couple of times, but I was always able to bring my emotions under control.

Until we got home...

I checked my e-mail and Jillian Lucas, a basketball player I coach who was at the party, had written the nicest letter to me. After fighting back tears all night long, what she wrote reduced me to an emotional mess. I grabbed my wife and just shook uncontrollably as I cried my eyes out on her shoulder. It was just too much for me to handle in one day.

Everyone should have a day like this in his or her life: A day where everything is right in the world. A day where you feel like you have made a difference in people's lives and they care enough to let you know that they love you. A day where you grow closer to those friends and family who have been there for you every step of the way. I am eternally grateful for everyone who made me feel loved, especially my wife and the Monroe family.

I've done a lot of thinking since this past weekend. I may have turned thirty. I may not be totally happy with what I've done with my life, as there are things I wish I could go back and do differently; I may have some regrets...

But I am a very blessed man...


*****

**Caleb Short Take**

Caleb and Connor attend a lot of high school girls' basketball games during each season. Connor will usually sit on Kristi's lap almost the entire game and watch with utter fascination as the players compete. Caleb, on the other hand, can't seem to sit still for a minute and has to be playing with his toys or other children who attend the game.

One particular night, a couple of boys about six or seven years old came up to Caleb and asked him if he wanted to go to the cafeteria with them. Kristi immediately told Caleb he couldn't go, and our son decided to throw a fit. Kristi sternly told him to knock it off, but Caleb was not to be denied his public display of disapproval. To make things worse, our good friend, Chuck Lucas, who takes a lot of photos at the games, began to tease Kristi by taking pictures of our five-year-old, as he threw the fit of his life. When he realized it was getting him nowhere, the fit subsided. Caleb looked up into Kristi's eyes, wiped the tears away and asked, "Mommy, what's a cafeteria?"

# And Then Some

"Brittnia's here!!" shouted Caleb and Connor in stereo sound as they saw our baby-sitter get out of her car and walk up the sidewalk to our house. Joyful dancing and a good test of our sofa's warranty followed as my two young boys jumped up and down, acting like Christmas morning was here once again. Caleb then ran to the door to let her in, while Connor continued to act as if he had just won a lifetime supply of candy. Kristi and I smiled as we watched the scene unfold before us—a scene that is repeated no matter how often Brittnia comes to our house. It also made us both realize how incredibly blessed we are to have her in our life.

I first met Brittnia Brandl when she walked into basketball practice during her freshman year of high school, and we got to know her a little better as each month went by. She soon took up permanent residency in our family's heart, and Kristi and I began to pray for Brittnia whenever we thought of her—which was often. I permanently bonded with her one particular afternoon during her sophomore year. Jamie Rusch, another basketball player at the time and I had gone to visit Brittnia in the hospital to cheer her up after her knee surgery. She was fresh out of the operating room and when we walked into the room, we were rewarded with a big smile, followed by a wave of vomiting. Yes, nothing shows your gratitude like stomach bile! She was very embarrassed but I reassured her that once a person throws up in front of another, they become friends for life!

As our lives became more entwined, I came to realize the quality that made Brittnia so special. Professor Richard Weaver once stated that what often sets a successful person apart from others are three simple words: "and then some." Brittnia figured this out a long time ago. When she was playing basketball for me, she worked hard, had a great attitude, loved and respected her teammates…and then some.

When she helps me videotape weddings for my video production business, she puts in a full day's work…and then some. She shows up earlier than expected, stays later than she needs to, and complains that we pay her too much money. She is the model employee.

However, nothing compares to how she is as a baby-sitter! She is trustworthy, dependable, responsible, goes out of her way to accommodate us...and then some!

The very first time Brittnia baby-sat for us, we knew we had someone special. From the time she walked in the door until the time she left our house, she gave our boys 100% of her time and attention. While some teenagers might be calling their boyfriends, watching TV, or doing their homework while they baby-sit, Brittnia spends her time playing hide-and-go-seek, tag, and reading countless books to my overactive children. She has role-played "The Lion King" so many times that I think she must secretly shudder at the name "Mufasa," as much as the hyenas do in the Disney movie! ("Mufasa! Mufasa! Mufasa!")

Many times as we walk up to our house while Brittnia is baby-sitting, we will pause outside of the window for a minute and watch her as she lovingly plays with, reads to, and cares for our two rambunctious boys. One night, just as we were leaving the house and our children in her capable hands, Caleb jumped on her back for a piggy-back ride. Kristi and I went to dinner, then stopped back at the house two hours later for something before we went to a movie. As we walked up to the door, we could see Brittnia walking around the living room with monkey-boy Caleb clinging to her back. I know better than to think that my boy had stayed there for the entire two hours, but I can honestly say that it wouldn't surprise me if it were true.

In all things in her life, Brittnia does what is expected of her...and then some. In the past four years she has earned our respect, our loyalty, and our love. We are extremely proud of our Brittnia for everything she does in her life, but never were we prouder than when we found out that she had committed her life to Christ toward the end of her freshman year. She shared with us that one night she went into her room, cried, and prayed for Jesus to come into her heart. She asked Him to take over her life because she needed help. She took all of the things she was dealing with at the time, and surrendered everything to Jesus. She became a new creation...

This past Sunday, Brittnia was baptized. She stood before family and friends and made a public profession of her faith in Christ. Kristi and I had been looking forward to sharing this important day with her since she first told us when she was getting baptized, a little over two months ago. We could just picture her beaming face as she would stare out over the crowd and make eye contact with those who love her dearly...Caleb, our five-year-old was so excited Sunday morning as we were getting ready to leave our house. "Daddy! We get to go see Brittnia get pushed in the water today, don't we?!" On the ride to Brittnia's church, Kristi and I explained to Caleb all about baptism and what it stands for in a believer's life. All of us were anticipating Brittnia's big day...

I dropped Kristi off at the door and then went to find a parking spot. I had Connor with me and when we walked into the sanctuary, I saw that the baptism had already started. A numbness crept into my heart. One of the few times in our life we thought we were early—twenty minutes early! I looked at Kristi and begged, "Please tell me that Brittnia hasn't been baptized yet?" She didn't answer right away, and my stomach turned to ice, because I knew from her silence that Brittnia had. It turned out that the baptism had started at 12:00 and not 12:30. Both of us had the time wrong and later when we got home, the invitation mocked us with the correct time.

There were fifteen to twenty believers being baptized that afternoon, and I sat there totally numb as the pastor finished up with the last seven or eight people. I wanted to cry. I wanted to ask the pastor if he could do it again. I wanted it all to be some kind of a bad dream that I could wake up from...

We had let our Brittnia down...

We had wanted to make eye contact with her, just before she walked to the baptismal and tell her that we loved her...

We had wanted to silently pray for her young life just as the pastor said, "I baptize you in the name of the Father, and the Son, and the Holy Spirit..."

We had wanted our two young sons to see Brittnia as she publicly let everyone know that four years earlier she asked Jesus to forgive her of her sins, come into her life, and had given total control of everything over to God. We had hoped that it might make an impression on them even at their early ages...

We had wanted to watch Brittnia's future husband, Jeff, as he also was baptized, and pray for their young relationship, that it might stay strong...

But it wasn't meant to be...

Jamie Rusch, who was sitting in front of me leaned back and whispered, "If it is any consolation, Brittnia's face got really red just before she was baptized." That made me smile, as everyone who knows Brittnia knows that she blushes easily...

Caleb, who was sitting on my lap, finally realized that it was over and that, as far a he could see, Brittnia hadn't been baptized yet. "Awwwwwwww! Brittnia didn't get dunked!!" he shouted.

We gave Brittnia a hug afterwards, wet hair and all, and she asked us if we got to see it. I had to tell her that we were about four minutes too late, and that we had the time mixed up. She reassured us that it was all right, but I felt my stomach tighten again into the kind of knots only an Eagle Scout could tie.

All day I asked, "Why God? Why did we have to miss this important day in our Brittnia's life?"

Even though we missed that moment, we wanted to share this with you today, on your nineteenth birthday, Brittnia:

Jesus will always be there for you. He never makes promises He can't keep and He is never, ever late in His timing. He will be your Friend when your friends fail you. He will be your Parent when your parents fail you. He will be your Husband when your future husband fails you, and he will fill the void that is in all of our lives like nothing else can...

Brittnia, Jesus will bless your life and provide for all of your needs, both emotionally and physically...and then some. He will comfort you when you are down, make your marriage work when there seems to be no hope, bless you with wonderful children, loving friends and family...and then some.

You could be our baby-sitter for the next twenty years. You could help me with my video business for the next fifty and be the perfect employee. You could have been born fourteen years later and ended up marrying Caleb and been the perfect daughter-in-law...but there is nothing, absolutely nothing, you could ever do that would top giving your life to Jesus as you have done. That makes us the happiest people on the face of the whole earth! No matter what happens the rest of our lives, no matter how close we may get to you, it all pales before the thought that we will get to spend the rest of eternity with our Brittnia.

We love you...and then some!

# Somebody Help the Boy!

I was hired to do a video for Clinton Middle School's annual class trip to Washington, DC this past year. Basically I capture the essence of the trip on videotape and then edit the four-day tour down to one hour for the students to relive the memories for years to come.

It was the second day of the trip and we were visiting the Supreme Court. I had all the footage I wanted for this leg of the journey and was just waiting for our group to move on to our next stop. I stood next to two of the chaperones while I waited for all the students to finish their tour of the Court House.

After a short while it occurred to me that everyone around me was unfamiliar. I looked to the left and to the right and didn't recognize anyone. I then went upstairs to see if our group was meeting there, but again saw no familiar faces. Finally, I asked a security guard if he had noticed where the school group went to, and he told me they left the building about ten minutes ago. I had no clue which door to exit, but he pointed out the exact door that they left through. I hurried out into the rain, with high hopes, thinking that the group would be waiting for me. It was not to be as once again I didn't recognize a single soul. Now I was getting worried. I didn't see my group, nor the buses that we came in.

To understand the dilemma that I was in you have to understand a little bit about me. You see, I am probably the most unorganized person on the face of the earth. I pay attention to details only when I feel that I need to. For example: I didn't know the name of the tour company we were touring with. I had no idea where we were supposed to be going next, nor did I even pay attention to the name of the hotel we were staying at. In fact, I didn't even know what city the hotel was in, as we were staying outside of the D.C. area.

There I was. Standing in the rain outside the Supreme Court, holding my $1500 video camera, hopelessly scanning the streets for a group of over a hundred middle school students and chaperones. I frantically tried to recall where we were supposed to go next, but again, I had not paid attention to the details. Losing a group of over a hundred people seemed pretty impossible to me, so I had not filed the necessary information away in my pea-sized brain.

I wasted a good five minutes or so standing in the rain, looking up and then down the street hoping to see a huge mass of 8th graders, or at least a bus that I recognized. But the longer I stared down the street, the wetter I got, and the more hopeless I felt.

"SOMEBODY PLEASE HELP THE BOY!!"

I nervously laughed to myself and realized that I was in trouble. I racked my gelatinous gray matter again, searching for a name, a place, or anything that might ring a bell and help me find my group, or at least a way back to the nameless hotel. But the harder I tried to remember, the more I realized I was up the D.C. crick without a paddle.

I tucked my expensive video camera under my light jacket to keep the rain off of it, and started walking down a side street that looked promising. My heart started beating faster as I thought of the headlines when they found me: "Country Hick found wandering back alleys of Washington, DC uttering, 'Somebody please help the boy!' with his last breath."

It was about this time that I started praying. "Lord, I know I got myself into this mess by not paying attention to what I was supposed to, but I am really starting to get worried now. Please help me to find my way back to my group."

I knew I was in a pretty hopeless situation, but gave my problem over to God and trudged on.

I had gone about seven or eight blocks down the street when I came upon a little old lady. As I walked up next to her and started to pass on the left, she asked, "So what are you doing with that video camera? Are you sight-seeing?"

I thought I had the video camera well under my jacket, but she saw it sticking out as I walked by. I am usually a pretty friendly person, but this was one time I didn't feel like striking up a conversation. I wanted to walk right on by pretending I didn't hear her, but I knew that I couldn't be that rude to her. I know most little old ladies are of the sweet type, usually being referred as, "That sweet little old lady," but she seemed like the extra sweet, sugary type.

"I'm here sight seeing with a group of students from Wisconsin, and I am the video guy who is capturing their trip for a memento," I said as I slowed down to her pace.

"Oh really!" she said. "That must be the group of kids that just about ran me over about ten minutes ago. There were hundreds of them!"

I came to an abrupt halt on the sidewalk.

"Are you kidding me? Did you really see a group of students?"

"Yep! They swarmed by me and were heading down that street over there."

"THANK YOU! THANK YOU! THANK YOU!" I said unashamedly. "I thought I'd lost them and have been looking for them for what seems like forever!"

"Well you better be on your way young man, and hurry if you want to catch them."

I thanked her a hundred or so more times, and then ran back in the opposite direction from which I was going, hope swelling in my bosom. (Whoa! I think that is the first time I have ever referred to my chest as a bosom!)

I still had no clue where I was going but at least now I knew I was going in the right direction. All the while I kept praying, first thanking God that he had sent the sweet, precious, little old lady to point me in the right direction, and then asking him to continue to provide guidance for me.

It was about then that I remembered we were scheduled to meet with Herb Kohl, our State Senator, later that day. I thought that if I could just find out where Senator Kohl was, I could at least meet up with my tour group some time in the next few hours.

Now instead of crying out, "SOMEBODY PLEASE HELP THE BOY!" It was more like, "DOES ANYBODY KNOW WHERE HERB KOHL LIVES!"

I spied a policeman on the street corner and went up to him, hoping that he didn't take me for a thief. I mean, here I was out of breath, and with an expensive video camera tucked under my jacket, like I had just robbed a sweet little old lady. I asked him if he could point me towards the building that Senator Kohl resided. He pointed to a larger building about three blocks up the street. I thanked him too, and off I went.

When I came to this building, I asked a security guard if this is where Senator Kohl would be and she stated that yes indeed, I had come to the right place. I was so excited that I almost didn't notice the security check just inside the door, and I was rather rudely reminded to place my video camera on the conveyor belt and then walk through the metal detector. When I passed the detector and had my precious video camera back in my possession, I asked the nice lady at the information desk if a large school group had recently passed through there. She told me that she didn't remember any school group coming through. I was disappointed, but clung to my only hope for a happy reunion with my fellow Wisconsinites.

"If a school group did come here to meet with Senator Kohl, where would they go," I asked politely.

"Go down this hall and turn to your right. You will see a huge lobby where he usually talks to the student groups that come through. You can wait there for them, if they come."

I practically floated down the hall to the lobby, hope still swelling in my bosom until I rounded the corner and saw a huge, but empty lobby.

"Stinkin' Stink!" I said, which is my usual statement of frustration. Although I was extremely glad to be there, I was really expecting God to work it out so that the group was there. I decided to bide my time and hope for the best.

I made my way around the corner of a huge metal structure in the middle of the lobby and found that the lobby was not only huge, it was enormous! I was only viewing half of the lobby from my vantage point. Oh yeah, and there was my tour group on the other side of the metal structure. They all had their backs turned to me as they waited patiently for Senator Kohl to make his appearance.

So I did what any other proud videographer who doesn't pay attention to details would have done. I slowly blended into the back of the group and pretended like I was never missing. And guess what? Nobody missed me!

The only one I told that day was Mr. Greer, my role model, and the teacher in charge of the trip. After a good laugh, he made sure he got me a bracelet from the tour company. It contained some details that I had overlooked. Namely, the tour company's name, its phone number, and the hotel we were staying at.

You just never know when you might need that information!

# The Boys of Iwo Jima

Each year my video production company is hired to go to Washington, DC with the eighth grade class from Clinton, Wisconsin where I grew up, to videotape their trip. I always enjoy visiting our nation's capitol, and each year I take some special memories back with me. But this fall's trip was especially memorable.

On the last night of our trip, we stopped at the Iwo Jima memorial. It is the largest bronze statue in the world and depicts one of the most famous photographs in history—the WWII image of the six brave men raising the American flag at the top of Mount Suribachi on the Island of Iwo Jima, Japan. About one hundred students and chaperones piled off the buses and headed toward the memorial. I noticed a solitary figure at the base of the statue, and as I got closer he asked, "Where are you guys from?"

"Wisconsin," I replied.

"Hey, I'm a Cheesehead, too! Come gather around Cheeseheads, and I will tell you a story."

James Bradley just happened to be in Washington, DC to speak at the memorial the following day. He was there that night to say goodnight to his dad, who has since passed away. He was just about to leave when he saw the buses pull up. I videotaped him as he spoke to us, and received his permission to share what he said from my videotape. It is one thing to tour the incredible monuments filled with history in Washington, DC but it is quite another to get the kind of insight we received that night. When all had gathered around he reverently began to speak.

"My name is James Bradley and I'm from Antigo, Wisconsin. My dad is on that statue, and I just wrote a book called Flags of Our Fathers which is #5 on the New York Times Best Seller list right now. It is the story of the six boys you see behind me. Six boys raised the flag."

That's when he pointed to the guy putting the pole in the ground and told us his name was Harlon Block. "Harlon was an all-state football player. He enlisted in the Marine Corps with all the senior members of

131

his football team. They were off to play another type of game, a game called 'war.' But it didn't turn out to be a game. Harlon, at the age of twenty-one, died with his intestines in his hands.

Bradley shared that detail with us because he said that generals stand in front of the statue and talk about the glory of war. "You guys need to know that most of the boys in Iwo Jima were seventeen, eighteen, and nineteen years old."

He pointed again to the statue. "You see this next guy? That's Rene Gagnon from New Hampshire. If you took Rene's helmet off at the moment this photo was taken, you would find a photograph in the webbing. A photograph of his girlfriend. Rene put that in there for protection, because he was scared. He was eighteen years old. Boys won the battle of Iwo Jima. Boys. Not men."

The next image on the statue was that of Sergeant Mike Strank, we learned. "Mike is my hero." Bradley exclaimed. "He was the hero of all these guys. They called him the 'old man' because he was so old. He was already twenty-four. When Mike would motivate his boys in training camp, he didn't say, 'Let's go kill the enemy' or 'Let's die for our country.' He knew he was talking to little boys. Instead he would say, 'You do what I say, and I'll get you home to your mothers.'"

The next man on the statue was Ira Hayes, a Pima Indian from Arizona who lived through the terror of Iwo Jima. "Ira Hayes walked off Iwo Jima. He went into the White House with my dad and President Truman told him, 'You're a hero.' He told reporters, 'How can I feel like a hero when 250 of my buddies hit the island with me and only twenty-seven of us walked off alive?'"

"So you take your class at school. 250 of you spending a year together having fun, doing everything together. Then all 250 of you hit the beach, but only twenty-seven of your classmates walk off alive. That was Ira Hayes. He had images of horror in his mind."

We learned that Ira Hayes died dead drunk, face down at the age of thirty-two, ten years after the famous photo was taken.

"The next guy, going around the statue, is Franklin Sousley from Hilltop, Kentucky, a fun-lovin' hillbilly boy," Bradley continued. "Franklin died on Iwo Jima at the age of nineteen. When the telegram came to tell his mother that he was dead, it went to the Hilltop General Store. A barefoot boy ran that telegram up to his mother's farm. The neighbors could hear her scream all night and into the morning. The neighbors lived a quarter of a mile away."

Finally Bradley pointed to the statue's image of his father, John Bradley from Antigo, Wisconsin. His dad lived until 1994, but declined all interviews. "When Walter Kronkite, or the New York Times would call, we were trained as little kids to say, 'No, I'm sorry sir, my dad's not here. He is in Canada fishing. No, there is no phone there, sir. No, we don't know when he is coming back.' My dad never fished or even went to Canada. Usually he was sitting right there at the table eating his Campbell's soup, but we had to tell the press that he was out fishing. He didn't want to talk to the press. You see, my dad didn't see himself as a hero. Everyone thinks these guys are heroes, 'cause they are in a photo and a monument. My dad knew better. He was a medic. John Bradley from Wisconsin was a caregiver. In Iwo Jima he probably held over 200 boys as they died, and when boys died in Iwo Jima, they writhed and screamed in pain."

Bradley recalled his third grade teacher calling the elder Bradley a hero. "When I went home and told my dad that, he looked at me and said, 'I want you always to remember that the heroes of Iwo Jima are the guys who did not come back. DID NOT come back.'"

"So that's the story about six nice young boys, Bradley finished. "Three died on Iwo Jima, and three came back as national heroes. Overall, seven thousand boys died on Iwo Jima in the worst battle in the history of the Marine Corps. My voice is giving out, so I will end here. Thank you for your time."

That number boggled my mind as I tried to comprehend how many lives those deaths altered back on American soil so many years ago. How many hearts of loved ones left behind were seared? Loved ones like this proud son who had so graciously shared part of his history with us.

Suddenly the monument wasn't just a big old piece of metal with a flag sticking out of the top. It came to life before our eyes through the heartfelt words of a son who did indeed have a father who was a hero then...and now.

# All is Well With the World Tonight

A husband takes his wife's hand and whispers, "Honey, take some time for yourself this evening. I started a bubble bath for you. Don't worry about the kids. I'll take care of getting them to bed..."

A high school student hugs her mom and dad tightly and says, "Thanks for making me do my homework this weekend instead of going out with my friends...I know I have a shot at that scholarship now, and I owe it all to both of you." She even offers to do the dishes before turning in early for bed...

An elderly gentleman is returning home from his nightly walk when four tough looking teenagers approach him. They walk slowly up behind him, grab him and say, "Sir. We just wanted you to know that you dropped your billfold a couple of blocks back. We are really sorry, but we were unable to get all the snow off your leather wallet. Here it is. Everything is still there. We're disappointed that we couldn't get all the moisture off it before it started to stain...No, we don't deserve any reward, we were just glad we came along when we did."

A lonely stray cat limps up to the dark house. He lifts his keen nose and sifts the cold air currents. There is food up ahead. He hasn't eaten in days, and he is cold and growing weaker by the hour...He has been here before and knows the dog chained to the doghouse will not let him near, but desperation drives him on. He draws closer to the appetizing aroma coming from the food dish, all the while waiting for the deep growling to begin. To his amazement he approaches the dish unchallenged and begins to gulp huge amounts of food. The Doberman only watches...When he is done eating and his hunger is satisfied, he hears the dog whine. The abandoned stray walks slowly up to the canine and they sniff noses. Soon they are fast asleep, sharing the warmth that only two can provide. For one night, the ancient enmity between cat and dog has been set aside...

A young single mom turns off the TV and walks slowly into the kitchen. She looks longingly at the bottle of whiskey on the counter...This is part of her evening ritual. It's how she deals with her problems. It's how she gets to sleep most nights, but for some reason tonight feels different. The tall bottle doesn't call to her as strongly. She doesn't feel the overwhelming urge to bring the container to her lips, to feel the fiery liquid burn down the back of her throat and make her forget...

Instead she gracefully slides over to the kitchen sink and pours every last drop down the drain. "Not tonight," she whispers to herself. Maybe not ever again...

She makes her way down the hallway and looks in on her sleeping children. She walks from bedside to bedside, bending down and gently planting a loving kiss on each round chubby cheek.

She is in bed before midnight for the first time in a year. She just might make it to work on time tomorrow. "Boy, won't my boss be surprised," she thinks to herself.

Just as she is drifting off to sleep, the stillness of the night is broken by the sudden, jarring ring of the phone. "Hello," she says sleepily. She can't believe what she is hearing. She doesn't want to believe. She thinks she is just going to wake up from this dream and none of it will be true. She reaches down and pinches her leg...She isn't dreaming. The voice on the other end of the phone belongs to her husband who left her two years ago. "Honey, I'm coming home, if you'll have me. I have made a lot of mistakes in my life and leaving you and the kids was the biggest..." She sobs quietly into the mouthpiece...

"Don't cry honey, everything is going to be all right from now on..."

Last night, after 95 long years, the Chicago Cubs finally win a play-off series by defeating the Atlanta Braves 5-1.

Yes, all is well with the world tonight...

Maybe all of these things didn't happen last night. Maybe Michael T. Powers just has an overactive imagination. Maybe...

Nah! The Cubbies win and all is well with the world!

# Eighteen Years Late

Junior high is probably the worst time in young people's lives. Bodies are changing in ways they never thought possible, and they spend most of their time trying to fit into a mold that peers have formed for them. Gone are the days of Elmer's glue, crayons, and the tiny scissors with the rounded edges. (Yes, they are trusted with the sharp-edged scissors in junior high.) From here on out, they have their own lockers, carry their books to each class, and start making their own decisions about which classes to take. Oh yeah, I almost forgot. They have to take showers in front of their peers! Naked!! AAARRRGHHH!!!!!!

What I remember most about junior high, however, was the incredible pain and heartache that students inflicted on one another with their words and actions. There were students who seemed to have it all together, and made those around them feel as if they didn't measure up. It wasn't until much later that I learned that those who ripped on others suffered from a terrible self-image, so in order to make themselves feel better, they tore others down. In fact, they were usually a totally different person from the one they presented to the outside world.

I didn't have the best self-image in junior high, and there were two things that I fell back on to be accepted: athletics and humor. I have always been a decent athlete, which brought a certain confidence and comfort level in my life, and I have always been able to make people laugh. At times the laughter came at another's expense, unfortunately, and most times I didn't fully realize what I was doing to the self-images of those around me, particularly one classmate of mine.

Her name was Tracy and she had a crush on me. Instead of nicely letting her know that I wasn't interested in her, I got caught up in trying to be funny, with her being the brunt of my jokes. I am ashamed now to think of how I treated her in seventh grade. I went out of my way to make things miserable for her. I made up songs about her, and even wrote short stories in which I had to save the world from Tracy the evil villain.

That all changed about half way through the year, however. Mr. Greer, my physical education teacher, came up to me one day.

"Hey, Mike, you got a second?"

"Sure, Mr. Greer!" I said. Everybody loved Mr. Greer, and I looked up to him like a father.

"Mike, I heard a rumor that you were going around picking on Tracy?"

He paused and looked me straight in the eye. It seemed like an eternity before he continued.

"You know what I told the person I heard that from? I told them it couldn't possibly be true. The Mike Powers I know would never treat another person like that. Especially a young lady."

I gulped, but said nothing.

He gently put his hand on my shoulder and said, "I just thought you should know that."

Then he turned and walked away without a backward glance, leaving me to my thoughts.

That very day I stopped picking on Tracy.

I knew that the rumor was true, and that I had let my role-model down by my actions. More importantly, though, it made me realize how badly I must have hurt this girl and others for whom I had made life difficult.

It was probably a couple of months later before I fully realized the incredible way in which Mr. Greer had handled the problem. He not only made me realize the seriousness of my actions, but he did it in a way that helped me to save some of my pride. My respect and love for him grew even stronger after that.

I don't think I ever apologized to Tracy for my hurtful words and actions. She moved away the next year, and I never saw her again. While I was very immature as a seventh grader, I still should have known better. In fact, I did know better, but it took the wisdom of my favorite teacher to bring it out into the light.

So, Tracy, if you're out there, I am truly sorry for the way that I treated you, and I ask for your forgiveness—something I should have done eighteen years ago.

# She's Earned It

Today I get to introduce a woman who has had a profound influence in my life: teacher Karen Mullen of Clinton High School in Clinton, Wisconsin. I recently had the great privilege of writing a letter to Wisconsin Senator Herb Kohl on Karen's behalf. She was nominated by one of her current students, Stacey Luety, for a statewide teaching award. One that is not necessarily based solely on years of service, although that is important. No, this particular honor deals more with how they have touched the lives of their students and what they have done for their communities and education in general.

If the following letter brings up memories of your favorite teachers, I would ask that you make an attempt to write to those men and women who have touched your life through their gift of teaching. Teachers do a thankless job for an obscenely low pay check, and many times there are no short term "rewards" as they must often wonder if they are getting through to their students. The simple act of a card or letter, even if you haven't seen them in twenty years, will allow them to realize that they have made a difference in the lives of their students. And hey, if you are currently a student, I'm sure it would be good for your high school or college career to let your present teacher know they are doing a good job! (That and a nice big shiny red apple!)

So without further ado, I give you: Mrs. Karen Mullen—a teacher who has made a difference!

*****

Dear Senator Kohl,

I have had the privilege of knowing Karen Mullen, first as a teacher, and now as someone I have chosen to edit my first book. There is no one who prepared me more for college than did Mrs. Mullen. She encouraged my love of reading and writing, developed a love for classic literature through her choice of authors to study, and gave me some life lessons that I will never forget.

We did not just read a textbook, do homework on it, and get tested on the material in her classes. We were allowed to have open discussion after each story, sometimes veering away from the subject matter at hand, but always pertaining to something that we as students were interested in. She was tough but fair and earned the respect if not the love of all her students.

Most classes in high school I breezed through with minimal amount of work. I rarely had any school work that I took home. Not that our teachers didn't push us, it was just that I was able to figure out most of what was going on and finish assignments while the teacher was still talking about them. That was until I had Mrs. Mullen. I was nudged, stretched and sometimes jolted out of my academic cruise control by her. For the first time in my high school career, I was working on assignments at home and most of those dealt with writing papers. We wrote papers, and then we wrote some more papers. I didn't appreciate her style of education until I got to college. After my first few weeks of university life, I was grateful for Mrs. Mullen. If it weren't for her classes in high school, college would have been a total shock for me.

Not only did she prepare me for college, she also changed my reading habits. Growing up, I had two genres that I read, and two only—epic fantasy, like the Lord of the Rings, and wildlife and outdoor fiction. When study hall came, I was usually caught up with my homework and would read for the entire period. During the first year I had her as a teacher in American Literature, I began to branch out and read the classics, but not just when we had an assignment. No, for the first time in my life I began to read Thoreau, Melville, and Poe for the pure pleasure of reading.

Towards the end of the first quarter of my senior year, my parents came to see Mrs. Mullen during one of the regularly scheduled parent/teacher conferences. I had straight A's that first quarter...or so I thought. There in front of Mrs. Mullen was a sheet of paper listing all the grades I was going to receive. Every teacher was giving me an A, except for Mrs. Mullen. She was giving me a B+ in her Psychological Literature class. Let me rephrase that. I was earning a B+ in her class. She told my folks that she felt bad that I wasn't going to get straight A's, but that I hadn't earned it. A B+, although close to an A, was still a B+.

My first thoughts were, "How much difference can there be between an A- and a B+. I was a good student, didn't get into trouble, and she couldn't give me an A, especially since straight A's would have been the result?" But the more I thought about it, the more I realized that I hadn't earned it, and that I would have to work harder the next quarter. That B+

stuck out like a sore thumb on my report card, but it was a motivating factor for me.

The following quarter, and the rest of my senior year, I earned straight A's. And the first one to come up and congratulate me was Mrs. Mullen after my second report card.

I leave you with a story I heard once that sums up my feelings toward my favorite high school teacher:

In ancient times a king decided to find and honor the greatest person among his subjects. A man of wealth and property was singled out. Another was praised for his healing powers; another for his wisdom and knowledge of the law. Still another was lauded for his business acumen. Many other successful people were brought back to the palace, and it became evident that the task of choosing the greatest would be difficult. Finally, the last candidate stood before the king. It was a woman. Her hair was white. Her eyes shown with the light of knowledge, understanding, and love.

"Who is this?" asked the king. "What has she done?"

"You have seen and heard all the others," said the king's aide.

"This is their teacher."

The people applauded and the king came down from his throne to honor her.

It is my hope that you also honor Karen Mullen. She's earned it.

Sincerely,
Michael T. Powers

Note from Michael: It is with great pleasure that I report that Mrs. Mullen did indeed win the coveted 2001 Kohl Foundation Teacher Award. Way to go Mrs. Mullen!

# Wild Day at Wrigley!

"I don't need anyone telling me when to cross the street," I yelled defiantly at the fourth grade Safety Patrol member. "I ain't no little kid, you know!" I said in my roughest, toughest ten-year-old voice. With that, I crossed the street and made my way home.

The next morning I was called to the principal's office. I was a bit scared, but I tried my best not to show it. "You know Mike, this is the third time I have had a complaint about you not obeying the Safety Patrols at the intersections." I said nothing in response. "The Safety Patrol members are there to make sure that no one gets hurt."

"I don't need anyone telling me when to cross the street. I'm not a two-year-old, you know."

"Mr. Powers, I don't care how old you are, or even think you are. You are going to start listening to and obeying the Safety Patrol, or you and I will be spending a lot of time together. Is that understood?"

I nodded and then was dismissed. I clenched my little fists together all the way out the door.

I was Public Enemy Number one to the Greenbrook Elementary School Safety Patrol. The brave young boys and girls who were sworn to help other students safely cross the street were told to be on the look out for me. The mere mention of my name made those fourth graders, who proudly wore the orange Safety Patrol vests, break out into a cold sweat.

It was soon after that, that I was approached by fellow fourth grader and captain of the Safety Patrol, Mike DiSalvo. I started to growl under my breath as he approached, and I prepared myself for an argument when he began to speak. "Hey, Mike! I've got a question for you. I noticed that you don't seem to need any help getting across the streets before and after school."

"That's right!" I barked back at him. "I'm not a two-year-old, you know?!"

"Well, Mike, since you are one of the few who don't need our help, I was wondering if you would like to join us? You know, become a member of the Safety Patrol. That way you can help all the other students get safely across the street."

The defensive reply I had planned froze on my lips and I stood there totally stunned. After what seemed like an hour I finally stammered, "Sure, I guess."

How could I turn down the Safety Patrol in their hour of need?

Within a few weeks I was the most devoted Safety Patrol member Greenbrook Elementary School ever had, and I wore my orange vest with pride. I showed up on my scheduled street corner ten minutes early each morning, and I didn't have a single problem with any of the students that I helped to cross the road each day. Well, except for the little second grader who told me one day, "I don't need anyone telling me when to cross the street. I'm not a two-year-old, you know." A quick talk with my mother and father later that night, though, took care of the problem, and my little brother never said that to me again.

I grew to love being in the Safety Patrol even more when, at the end of the year, we were rewarded for our service with a trip to Wrigley Field to watch my favorite baseball team, the Chicago Cubs. Most any boy who grew up in the Chicago area spent half their childhood playing baseball in the neighborhood lot, pretending they were Cub players Bill Buckner or Dave Kingman. The other half of their life was spent in front of the tube watching the Cubs play on WGN-TV. However, to actually get to go to a Cubs game in person was a dream come true!

The date was May 17, 1979, and the Cubs were taking on the Philadelphia Phillies. Our group of elementary school students got our first glimpse of heaven, as we looked out over historic Wrigley Field from the bleachers in right-center field. There are no words to describe the feeling that this fourth grader had at that time. The wind was blowing out that day and we settled in for an experience we would all remember for the rest of our lives...

The Phillies scored seven runs in the first inning and sent starting Cub pitcher, Dennis Lamp, to the showers before he even worked up a sweat. However, my beloved Cubs came right back with six runs of their own, and at the end of the first inning the score was 7-6. We knew then this was not going to be a normal Major League baseball game.

The Phillies went on to score eight runs in the third inning and built a 17-6 lead, and things weren't looking too bright for my Cubbies. However, my favorite player, Dave Kingman, was belting homers every other at-bat, and my second favorite player, Bill Buckner, hit a grand slam right into our group of Safety Patrol members. At the end of nine innings the game was miraculously tied, 22-22.

In the top of the tenth, Mike Schmidt hit his second homer of the game off Cub reliever Bruce Sutter to put the Phillies ahead 23-22. I wasn't worried though, as Kingman, who already had three home runs, was coming to bat for us in the bottom of the tenth. I remember standing up with the rest of the Cub faithful, pointing towards the left field bleachers, and shouting at the top of my little lungs, "NUMBER 4! NUMBER 4!" in the hopes that he would tie the game again with one swing. Rawley Eastwick, the fifth Phillies pitcher of the day, sent his best fastball hurtling towards home plate. Kingman took a mighty swing, and, with the crack of the bat, we all knew the game was going to be tied. His towering shot went high into the air and began its long decent towards the bleachers in left field... However, the ball fell just short, as did the Cubs' hopes of winning that day.

The game featured eleven home runs, fifty hits, and set many Major League records. More importantly, though, it was a magical day that all of us kids will never, ever forget...especially me. If it weren't for a fourth grader named Mike DiSalvo who was wise far beyond his years, I would not have been there that day to experience my first Cubs game.

I have lost track of my childhood friends since we moved to Wisconsin back in 1980. However, my guess is that Mike DiSalvo is the CEO of some Fortune 500 company, and that he regularly gives out Cub tickets to schools to be used by the brave young boys and girls of the Safety Patrol.

# Celebration of Life

On my way home from coaching basketball yesterday, I was listening to WGN, my favorite talk radio station out of Chicago. I could tell right away that there was something wrong by the somber mood of the speaker. There had been a plane crash. Two small planes collided into each other over a northern suburb of Chicago. What made the story hit close to home was that Bob Collins, the morning show man for WGN, was the pilot of one of the planes and had been killed. I'm sure that many readers have tuned in "Uncle Bobby" on their car radios in the Midwest. Later that night, as I made my forty-minute drive to my third shift job, I listened as the station reminisced and paid tribute to a man who was loved by many. They told story after story, describing him as the ultimate friend and a man who had lived life to the fullest. Genuine love and affection poured in from all over the country. The more I listened to how this man had influenced those around him, the more discouraged I became.

Why you ask?

I was discouraged because I wanted to know why we as a culture wait until somebody has passed away before we tell him or her how much we love them. Why do we wait until someone's ears can't hear before we let them how much they mean to us? Why do we wait until it is too late before we recall the good qualities of a person? Why do we build someone up after they have gone into eternity? What good does it do then?! We share memory after memory, as we laugh, cry, and think back about what was positive in a person's life. Yes, it does help us cope with the grief of losing someone who was special to us, and, yes, it does bring those who are coping closer together. Unfortunately, as we lovingly remember this person, our words fall short of the ears that most needed to hear them.

Just once I would like to see a celebration of life instead of a gathering of death. A celebration where stories are told, eyes mist over, laughter rings out, and as the speaker concludes his or her loving tribute, the person they are honoring rises from their chair and gives them the biggest bear hug! Wouldn't that be something! The special people get to hear the stories and come to the realization that they have made a difference on this earth, and all this is done well before they leave their earthly bodies and go into eternity. When the inevitable funerals finally come, we can say good-bye with the knowledge that they knew exactly how people felt about them while they were here on earth.

I now have a stronger resolve to tell those around me how much they mean to me. I am going to let my wife know just how loved and appreciated she is, not only by my words, but also by my actions. I am going to play Batman with my four-year-old more often, and in the middle of our romping, I am going to grab him, hug him tightly, and tell him how thankful I am that he is my son. I am going to sneak into my sleeping toddler's bedroom, place my lips on his chubby cheek, and thank God for the bundle of joy He has brought into my life. Each day I will make a point to tell both of my boys how much I love them, whether they are four or eighteen! From there, I am going to let family and friends know the tremendous impact they have had on my life. Finally, I am going to let the high school players I coach know that I look forward to each and every minute that I get to spend with them in the gym.

Do you love someone? Then tell them! Has someone been an influence in your life? Then give them a call! Has someone made a difference in your life? Then write them a letter or send them an e-mail! Don't let another day go by without letting that person know. There is something special about a written letter that expresses feelings of love towards another. I don't know about you, but I have letters and cards from people that I have saved for years, and from time to time, I get them out and reread them. They can turn a depressing day into one where I realize just how blessed and lucky I am.

Life is too short to leave kind words unsaid. The words you say, or the letter you write, might just make all the difference in the world.

# Words of Wisdom

Words of wisdom from a friend touched my life so profoundly that I had to share them... share them in the hopes that there is another "Michael" out there who needs to hear these words too...

A few years ago I was very, very frustrated. I wanted to write stories but everything else in my life kept getting in the way. At the time I was thinking about putting my stories together in a book, but there were also many stories in my head that I could not find the time to sit down and write. I was working a third shift job (with a forty minute commute each way) and running my video production company out of my house so that Kristi could stay home with our boys, all the while trying to balance family time along with a passion for writing...

As my frustration grew, I wrote a letter to my friend, author Joan Wester Anderson, and explained how frustrated I was and how I wished and hoped that God would just let me drop everything and become a full time writer... I told her about how guilty I felt about wanting to spend more time with my wife and children and kept thinking that if God would just make me a full time writer I could find the time to do so...

Here was an author with millions of books in print—she would understand my frustration and tell me to go ahead and quit my jobs, pursue my writing career, and let God worry about how the bills would be paid...

Boy, did I need to hear the pearls of wisdom she sent back my way... and I share them with all of you with her permission. May you be touched by her words and may we all be challenged to take a long hard look at our priorities in life.

I love you Joan and I thank you for always being there for me.
Michael

Dear Michael,

Please take it from a person who has been there—you can do anything in life again, or later, anything but raise your children. When our five were small, we had periods of debt that I thought were so huge, they would squeeze me to death. I thought we would never get out from under, much less take a decent vacation, etc. But we both stuck to our beliefs that our children needed to be raised by both of us. I started a little writing business on the side (how well God provides—little did I know how big it would grow someday) and my husband's up-and-down commission work continued to flounder. But we knew where our kids were, who their friends were, when they appeared a bit "strange" (a situation to investigate), who was teaching them, what was being taught, you name it, we knew it. Our house was always open to their friends, and I actually learned a lot from those kids too.

What was the upshot? I hate to brag but I will—five absolutely wonderful adults, all spiritual, all moral, all loving us their parents intensely, and planning to leave the world a better place than they found it. Lots of family get-togethers with lots of laughter and reminiscing (next weekend we'll all travel to Washington DC to surprise one of our sons for his birthday—last month we met here for my mother's 90th birthday. No one would have dreamed of missing it.) My cup runs over, due to the seeds we planted during those early and very crucial days.

And I'm still not on Medicare!

You see, the point being missed by today's society is this: quality time is defined by a child as when he needs his mom or dad, not when his parent can schedule the time for him. A child's quality time doesn't and can't occur on a schedule. What about the times when you have to drop everything and walk a child back to return a candy bar he just stole from the supermarket? What about the time a child seems just a little too excited, and you sense—without knowing exactly why—that he's involved in something questionable. Parenting by Proxy (as Dr. Laura so beautifully points out) just doesn't work. And all those little teaching moments are gone forever.

We opted to raise our kids ourselves, and a funny thing happened. All the dreams I deferred, eventually got satisfied—when the time was better and I had more energy to devote to them. All the debts got paid, too, and if my husband and I keep our health, we will be able to afford some really wonderful trips and adventures. I have a spirit of complete comfort, no regrets at all, because I did what needed to be done at the right time. Best of all, my married son and his wife, primarily due to the example both families set, have opted to live the same way with their daughter. They are both self-employed by choice, and they work around her, so that one of them is always taking care of her. She is seven now and, according to her teacher, the best-adjusted child in her class. (Is this a coincidence?) And the seeds of the next generation are sown.

So Michael, I think your intuition (or maybe it's the Holy Spirit?) may be prompting you to defer your book for a while, along with those other things that aren't mandatory, and spend more precious hours with your family. The book will be there later (or, if it really nags, you can set up a few hours each week to work on your own projects, but NO MORE THAN THAT for now). If you put first things first, and by the way, that begins with a short period of prayer first thing every morning, God will find you all the time you need to do the things He wants you to do.

Sorry about ranting this way—but I just had to do it!!

Sincerely,
Joan Wester Anderson


Joan's words hit me like a Mack truck. I knew that God was speaking through her to send me a message and I started putting her words of wisdom into practice. I would love to be able to tell you that God worked out all my hopes and dreams the very next week but He didn't. However, as the months went by I found bits and pieces of time to write my stories without compromising time with my family. Slowly but surely I learned to say "No" to people when I knew I wouldn't have time to do what they were asking of me. I even began to say "No" to those video jobs that I knew would demand a great amount of time and stress both myself and my family to a breaking point...

Little by little my dream of having my own book came into focus; and then became a reality.

Then, as if God hadn't blessed me enough, I was able to walk away from my third shift job and accept a full time job with our church working with youth and producing videos to supplement the sermon topic each week. Not only does this job enable me to put all my time and energy into something that will make a difference for eternity, but I get to work out of my home and spend more time with my family. Now instead of rushing out of the house at my children's bedtime, to make a forty-minute drive to work, I get to snuggle with them on the couch and read them bedtime stories—Something I haven't been able to do since they were born...

Oh yeah... I forgot to mention that it has been a long time since I have written a new story and it doesn't bother me in the least bit!

God is good, all the time!

End Note From Michael: Be sure to visit Joan's website at: www.joanwanderson.com where you can join her weekly e-mail list and read excerpts from her New York Times best-selling books!

# Because We Care

Please take a moment to read the verses on the next page. We care about you, but we care even more deeply about where you will spend eternity. If you have never come to the point in your life where you have invited Jesus Christ into your life to be your Lord and Savior, then please consider doing that today.

We both came to know the Lord when we were younger; myself at the age of five and Kristi at the age of fourteen. When we did invite Christ into our hearts, we both prayed a prayer similar to the one below:

Dear Jesus,

I know that I am sinner and that I have not lived my life in a way that honors You. I believe that You are the Son of God and that Your death on the cross was a payment for my sins. I believe that You rose from the dead and that You are alive today preparing a place in heaven for those who trust in You. Please forgive me of my sins and come into my life as Savior and Lord. I am tired of trying to live life my way and I give control of that over to You. Help me to turn away from how I lived before and begin growing in knowledge about You.

Thank you for coming into my life, taking the punishment for my sins, forgiving me, and giving me eternal life in Heaven with You someday.

In Jesus' name, Amen.

The words above are not magical, nor do they have any power by repeating them word for word. Rather, Jesus would like you to pray to Him in your own heartfelt words...

If you just prayed right now and sincerely asked Jesus to forgive your sins and come into your life as Lord and Savior, then He is living inside you right now. 2 Corinthians 5:17 says, "Therefore, if anyone is in Christ, he is a new creation; the old has gone, the new has come!" Know that

He will never leave you or forsake you, and that there is nothing that can ever separate you from His love.

We hope that our writing has touched your heart in some way...but more importantly, we hope to meet you face to face in heaven someday!

Love,
Michael & Kristi

**For all have sinned and fall short of the glory of God.
– Romans 3:23**

**For the wages of sin is death, but the gift of God is eternal life through Jesus Christ our Lord. – Romans 6:23**

**But God demonstrates His love for us in this: while we were still sinners, Christ died for us. – Romans 5:8**

**Here I am! I stand at the door and knock. If anyone hears my voice and opens the door, I will come in and eat with him, and he with me. – Revelation 3:20**

**If you confess with your mouth, "Jesus is Lord," and believe in your heart that God raised him from the dead, you will be saved. For it is with your heart that you believe and are justified, and it is with your mouth that you confess and are saved. – Romans 10:9,10**

**Everyone who calls on the name of the Lord will be saved. – Romans 10:13**

# Who Are Michael And Kristi Powers?

Michael and Kristi have been married for sixteen years and both have a heart for teenagers. They have been involved in youth ministry for the past eighteen years and believe that one's outlook on the youth of today all depends on whether one thinks teenagers have problems, or are problems. They believe the former.

Kristi is a human development specialist...in other words a mommy! She helps Michael run his home-based business: Video Imagery, but most of her time is spent taking care of her four boys: Michael, the taller one, and Caleb, Connor, and Chase, the shorter ones. Her stories appear in six inspirational books, including the Chicken Soup for the Soul and Stories from the Heart series of books. She is homeschooling her children and in her spare time (yeah, right!) likes to curl up with a good book, travel, and spend time with family and friends.

Michael is the Youth Pastor at Faith Community Church in Janesville, Wisconsin, and owns and operates Video Imagery, a video production business that produces family memory videos (transferring photos and home movies over to video), corporate video, sports music videos, and weddings.

He is a Federation of Outdoor Volleyball Men's Open Sand Doubles Champion and an eight-time Gold Medallist in volleyball for the Badger State Games (Wisconsin's State Olympics). He is also a high school girls' basketball coach, and a certified USA Junior Olympic Girls' 18 and under volleyball coach.

Michael is an avid reader (he always has a good book going) and enjoys spending time with his family camping, fishing, and hiking.

Michael's stories have appeared in numerous newspapers and magazines around the world and in twenty different inspirational books including many in the Chicken Soup, Stories for the Heart, God Allows U-Turns, and God's Way series of books.

His future writing plans include a wildlife outdoor adventure novel for his three boys, a second book of true stories from his life, and a book on coaching that he would like to co-author with his mentor and hero, Bill Greer.

Michael and Kristi would love to hear from you!  Feel free to let them know what you thought of this book or perhaps comment on how a particular story may have touched your heart!   E-mail Michael at: HeartTouchers@aol.com and Kristi at: NoodlesP29@aol.com. You can write to them at:

Michael and Kristi Powers
Faith Community Church
2931 Lucerne Dr.
Janesville, WI 53545

Michael is also a motivational speaker, and can be scheduled for your next adult or teen event by contacting him at: HeartTouchers@aol.com.

# Become A HeartTouchers.com Member!

Come be a part of something special as we touch lives via e-mail! HeartTouchers.com is a free weekly E-zine that contains inspirational stories and poetry by published writers and the means to contact them via e-mail with your feedback. Each story is followed by quotes that will amuse, challenge, and inspire you. To join our weekly e-mail family, send an e-mail to: HeartTouchers@aol.com and ask to be added to the lists or visit: www.HeartTouchers.com and sign up from our website!

Fix yourself a soothing beverage, turn your computer on, and then sit back and let your stressful world fade away as you are encouraged and inspired by some of the best stories on the Internet! You will be blessed with hope, filled with laughter, and you may even shed a few good tears. But we promise that you will go away with a spring in your step and new outlook on this thing called life...

Check out our inspirational website to read all the past stories we have run: www.HeartTouchers.com

**Still not convinced? Here is what some of our members have been saying:**

"I can't remember who first forwarded a Heart Touchers e-mail to me, but I owe that person many thanks. I have since grown to love and appreciate you and Kristi through the stories you have written and the type of stories by other authors you have chosen to print. I look forward to each e-mail as a letter from good friends. These letters have truly been a blessing to me as, I'm sure, they have been to your thousands of subscribers. Keep up the good work!!"
—Charlene Kephart, California

"I have probably subscribed/unsubscribed to a hundred lists in the past couple of years—and I have almost never sent a thank you to any of them, but I wanted you to know how much I am enjoying yours. Please keep up the wonderful work. You are making a real difference in the lives of people you will never see, including me! I am at a place in my life where I need to feel uplifted and some sense of hope, and you are my source of both."
—Helen Bowles

"Everything you send is appreciated so much, and your writings are priceless. You truly have a gift and with this gift you touch so many hearts and souls. You make my day every time I turn my computer on. Thank You!"
—Billie Ward

"I have never made it a habit to respond or send my review on stories featured on your list, but your story touched me so much. I feel like I got it just at the right time, as if God is saying something to me, maybe telling me that I am not alone and I therefore need not feel alone 'cause I'm not. Since I subscribed to Michael's mailing list I have never been the same. I guess that only goes to prove that no one comes into contact with the Lord and still become the same and it makes me feel that God is so awesome and can work His wonders even through an ordinary e-mail!! I have learned to take my dreams, desires and aspirations to the one who knows my tomorrow because I am a mere mortal and do not know what tomorrow holds for me.

To you Michael, I only wish blessings upon you and your family only God knows the depth from which I say this. From stories I have read about you and Kristi you have made me believe that there is a thing called love somewhere out there. May the good Lord keep using you to touch the hearts of a million others!!" Love always,
—VNP - Johannesburg (South Africa)

Come join us!  A source of encouragement and inspiration is just an e-mail away!

HeartTouchers@aol.com or visit: http://www.HeartTouchers.com

# Become A Heart4Teens.com Member!

Heart4Teens.com is a brand new inspirational list just for teens!

This inspirational list for teenagers is run by popular Chicken Soup Authors Michael and Kristi Powers who have been involved in youth ministry for eighteen years!

Are you feeling overwhelmed with everything that life has thrown your way and are you looking for answers to tough questions about life and or God? Maybe you just want to be encouraged as you struggle through life as a teenager? We want you to know that there is hope and a bright future for you!

"For I know the plans I have for you," declares the LORD, "plans to prosper you and not to harm you, plans to give you hope and a future." —Jeremiah 29:11

This weekly list contains heart-touching stories, quotes, links to uplifting websites, and humor geared towards the teenage crowd. However, parents of teens, grandparents, college students, youth pastors, teachers, coaches, and anyone who just can't read enough inspirational stories will also benefit!

What are you waiting for?! Subscribe today and join the thousands of teens who receive inspirational stories and encouragement each week via e-mail!

Send an e-mail to Heart4Teens@aol.com and asked to be added to the list or visit: www.Heart4Teens.com and subscribe through our website!

## Visit the Heart4Teens.com website for information and answers to these teenage issues:

**How Do You Know God?** — Do you really know who God is? Did you know that He has a plan for your life? Would you like to have a loving relationship with the One who not only created you, but the entire universe?

**Having Thoughts of Suicide?** — Are you dealing with suicidal thoughts or have you tried to commit suicide?

**Are You Pregnant?** — Are you a teenager who finds herself pregnant? Are you a teenage guy and your girlfriend just told you she is pregnant? What do you do?

**Are You Considering an Abortion?** — You are a teenage girl and you find yourself faced with one of the biggest decisions of your life: "Do I have my baby or do I abort it?"

**Do You Have a Drug or Alcohol Problem?** — Find out more information on how you can get help with your drug and alcohol problem!

**Are Your Parents Getting a Divorce?** — If your parents are going through a divorce or if you have been living in a divorced family for years, we have info that will help you cope!

**Do You or a Friend Have an Eating Disorder?** — If you or a friend are dealing with an eating disorder, or if you want to know if you have an eating disorder, then we can help!

**Are You Dealing with the Death of a Family Member or Friend?** — Have you had to face the death of a family member or friend recently? We have answers to the questions you may have!

**Are You Being Abused?** — Are you being physically or sexually abused?

**Are You Dealing with Peer Pressure?** — Your peers are a powerful force in molding and shaping who you are. Are they pressuring you into situations that you would really rather avoid?

**What's the Big Deal About Premarital Sex?** — Answers to many of your questions about love and sex!

**Are You Battling Depression?** — Depression is bearing down on you like a huge boulder. Where Do You Turn?

**The Creation-Evolution Debate** — Does science back up God's Word? How can you intelligently discuss the Creation-Evolution debate with your peers and teachers? How do you react to your teacher or other students who believe in evolution?

**Miracles and Science** — Does Science disprove the miracles recorded on the Bible?

**Separation of Church and State** — Was "separation of church and state" the intent of America's founding documents and our founding fathers?

**Find answers to these problems and more on the Heart4Teens.com website!**

# Heart Touchers Books

If Heart Touchers is not available at your local bookstore you can order copies of our book by visiting: www.HeartTouchers.com. Credit Card orders and Pay Pal orders are accepted. Or you can make a check or money order for $13.95 (We'll pay shipping costs!) out to Michael T. Powers and send it to:

Michael T. Powers
Faith Community Church
2931 Lucerne Dr.
Janesville, WI 53545

Be sure to let us know who you would like it autographed for and then allow about two weeks for us to sign it and send it on its way to you.

Autographed copies of many of the other inspirational books that Michael and Kristi have stories in are also available through the HeartTouchers.com website. How cool would it be to be able to buy books like those in the Chicken Soup series for your friends and family with a personalized autographed message by one of the contributing authors! Included are a number of books just for teenagers. Do you have a teenage son, daughter, grandchild, friend of the family, Sunday school student, player that you coach, etc. that you want to touch in a life-changing way? This is the perfect opportunity. Teenagers are reading these books as fast as they can get their hands on them. Why? Because they are searching for meaning in their lives...and these books can provide direction.

For more information visit: www.HeartTouchers.com/books

Printed in the United States
65177LVS00002B/1-108